TWAYNE'S WORLD AUTHORS SERIES

A Survey of the World's Literature

GERMANY

Ulrich Weisstein, Indiana University

EDITOR

Christian Morgenstern

TWAS 508

Christian Morgenstern

CHRISTIAN
MÖRGENSTERN

By ERICH P. HOFACKER

Washington University, St. Louis

TWAYNE PUBLISHERS
A DIVISION OF G. K. HALL & CO., BOSTON

Copyright © 1978 by G. K. Hall & Co.

Published in 1978 by Twayne Publishers,
A Division of G. K. Hall & Co.
All Rights Reserved

Printed on permanent/durable acid-free paper and bound
in the United States of America

First Printing

Library of Congress Cataloging in Publication Data

Hofacker, Erich, 1898–1976.
  Christian Morgenstern.

  (Twayne's world authors series ; TWAS 508)
  Bibliography: p. 141–44
  Includes index.
  1. Morgenstern, Christian, 1871–1914.
2. Poets, German—19th century—Biography.
PT2625.064Z74   831'.9'12   78-18791
ISBN 0-8057-6349-X

For my sister Ilse

Contents

About the Author

Erich P. Hofacker was for many years Professor of German at Washington University in St. Louis and served also as chairman of the department. Prior to that he taught at the University of Pittsburgh, at Rutgers and at Yale. He received his Ph.D. from Tübingen (Germany), where he first encountered Rudolf Steiner's anthroposophy and the poetry of Christian Morgenstern. He has published extensively in the modern period, including a number of articles on Morgenstern. He has also written and co-authored several textbooks for elementary and intermediate German, including the very successful *Complete College German,* published by D. C. Heath & Co.

Preface

This is the first monograph in English on Christian Morgenstern, his life, and his work. Morgenstern is widely known as the creator of a grotesque kind of poetry all his own. But his contribution to the history of German poetry includes also serious lyrics of great charm, depth, and beauty. August Closs says in his well-known book *The Genius of German Lyric* that "Christian Morgenstern seeks to find a spiritual meaning in earthly life. His poetry and pensées, especially toward the end of his short life, turn towards mysticism."[1] It will be shown that his last, the anthroposophical, phase of his work constitutes a natural climax in the evolution of his ideas and their artistic expression.

This monograph is based primarily on Morgenstern's works and letters. In its biographical parts, it is greatly indebted to the standard work by Michael Bauer and Margareta Morgenstern, the poet's widow.[2] The English translations of the original passages and poems are my own. Both the chronology and the biography are based on the corresponding sections in Martin Beheim-Schwarzbach's monograph.[3] The conclusion attempts to demonstrate Morgenstern's increasing popularity with educated readers, which makes his work a significant ingredient of present-day German culture.

ERICH P. HOFACKER

POSTSCRIPT

In May, 1976, the author, my father, died suddenly; except for certain revisions, this book was ready for publication. He wrote it in order that others might better understand and enjoy a poet whose works he himself had loved since his student days at Tübingen. I have acted on his behalf in completing the final version of the manuscript. This has involved, in some cases, the augmentation of the author's literal translations of the "Gallows Songs" with freer renditions by Max Knight. [4]

ERICH P. HOFACKER, JR.

University of Michigan

Chronology

1900   *Ein Sommer.* September, Morgenstern goes to Davos (Switzerland) to recuperate.

1901   Spends the spring and summer near Lake of Lucerne, the winter in Arosa (Switzerland).

1902   Trip to Italy: Milan, Rapallo, Portofino, Florence, return to Switzerland. December, goes to Rome. *Und aber ründet sich ein Kranz.*

1903   March, travels to Fiesole near Florence; May, returns to Berlin; becomes reader for Bruno Cassirer (publisher) and editor of *Das Theater.*

1905   July, journeys to the island of Föhr. *Galgenlieder.* Spends winter in Birkenwerder near Berlin, begins *Tagebuch eines Mystikers,* reads Dostoevski.

1906   *Melancholie;* spends summer in Tirol, winter in Obermais near Merano. Reads Hegel, Fichte, Spinoza, Tolstoy.

1907   Takes trip to Lake Garda at Easter, returns to Switzerland.

1908   Goes to Berlin in spring; spends vacation in Dreikirchen, Tirol; meets Margareta Gosebruch von Liechtenstern; stays in Merano in the fall, travels to Freiburg to see Margareta in the hospital. October, goes to Strasburg; November, returns to Berlin; becomes engaged to Margareta.

1909   Hears lectures by Rudolf Steiner in Berlin; April, travels to Düsseldorf und Koblenz to hear Steiner; May, becomes member of the Anthroposophical Society. Attends lectures by Steiner in Oslo, Budapest, Kassel, Munich. August, visits his father in Silesia. Returns to Obermais, becomes seriously ill.

1910   March 7, marries Margareta. *Palmström, Einkehr.* May–August, stays in Bad Dürrenstein. September–October, Munich. Travels to upper Italy and Sicily. November becomes seriously ill in Taormina (Sicily).

1911   Spends three weeks in the German Hospital in Rome in the spring; moves to Arosa (Switzerland). *Ich und Du.*

1912   Receives honorary stipend from the German Schiller Society. August, goes to a sanitarium in Davos. October, meets Steiner in Zürich; returns to Arosa.

1913   Travels to Portorose in spring, stays there for two months, meets Michael Bauer. Goes to Bad Reichenhall (Bavaria) and Munich. November, trip to Stuttgart for a Morgenstern festival. Hears Steiner in Leipzig, and his own works recited by Marie von Sivers.

1914   Stays in sanitarium in Gries near Bolzano. Transfers to private quarters in Untermais near Merano; dies on March 31. *Wir fanden einen Pfad.*

CHAPTER 1

Childhood and Adolescence

CHRISTIAN Morgenstern's life span exactly coincides with the longest period of peace in modern German history. The poet was born in Munich on May 6, 1871, four days prior to the signing of the peace treaty that ended the Franco-Prussian War; he died in Untermais near Merano (Switzerland) on March 31, 1914, four months before the outbreak of World War I. He established himself as a literary critic in the capital of the new German Empire. That is the place from which he drew his modest economic subsistence as a contributor to literary journals, translator, publisher's reader, and as a poet in his own right. But only for short periods could he return to Berlin, with its ambitious literary life, because his lungs forced him to spend the greater part of his life outside of Germany, mainly in Switzerland. An independent thinker relentlessly searching for the meaning of life, he saw in the materialism of his day the principal foe of mankind. He sensed the catastrophe toward which the intellectuals of his time were drifting. A kind fate saved him from witnessing the violent collapse of the old order and granted him the opportunity to become the poet of a new spirituality.

Morgenstern was the first and only child of a happy young artist couple that adored him and showered tender affection upon him during the first decade of his life. If present-day psychology stresses the significance of the earliest years for the development of the personality, it can find an example in Christian Morgenstern. It is doubtful whether the poet could have endured the crippling effects of his lingering illness with such serenity and without any trace of bitterness if the happy circumstances of his early childhood had not nurtured his extravagant imagination and allowed it to flourish beyond the restraints which most children encounter. The boy was

15

named after his grandfather, Christian Morgenstern (1805–1867), a landscape painter of some renown and himself the son of a painter of miniatures. The poet's father, Carl Ernst Morgenstern (1847–1928), married the daughter of Joseph Schertel under whom he had studied landscape painting. Thus the seven-year-old boy took it for granted that he would follow in his father's footsteps.

The alternate stimulation of city life and living in the country offered an exceptionally wide range of experiences for the boy. In the spring his father would leave his villa on the outskirts of Munich to pursue his profession in the more picturesque regions of Bavaria. Wife and child would be taken along. The congenial artistic atmosphere of his parental home in Munich, with its many guests, and the contrasting life in the country, close to nature, where the imaginative child was often left to himself and could create a world of his own, constituted an ideal background for a happy childhood. The child's innate gentleness and his extremely sensitive conscience made it easy for his loving parents to guide him. Thus we can readily understand why the thirty-seven-year-old poet, aware of the lasting impact of these early years, could say that he was still living on the sunshine of his childhood. To be sure, the lack of systematic training was a serious drawback. Due to the frequent change of residence during the warmer months of the year, the boy's primary education was quite haphazard, left, as it was, to an occasional tutor or restricted to a few weeks' attendance in a village school. His father had his artistic interests and his mother was less and less able to devote her energy to Christian's education, as her progressive tubercular condition continued to undermine her vitality. She died when the boy was nine years old. Her death marked the end of his harmonious, carefree childhood. However, the mature poet, contemplating his life in retrospect, came to realize that the spiritual force emanating from his mother after her death had accompanied and guided him unswervingly through spiritual crises and frustrations until death lost its sting and the world had regained its God-given meaning for him.[1] A pious but undogmatic Catholic, she had instilled in her child an attitude of reverence and prayer.

The boy's education was further disrupted when his father gave up his Munich residence and moved to the little village of

Starnberg, where the local school proved to be quite primitive. The loving care and training which Christian received at the hands of a sympathetic governess, an artist's daughter, lasted only a few weeks. His father, searching for another solution, was relieved when Christian's godfather, the Hamburg art dealer Otto Meyer, was willing to take the boy into his family. We know, through a letter from the daughter of the house, about the ten-year-old's interest in songs, his attempts at writing stories and verse, and his inclination to tease, which may have been a disguised way of establishing affectionate communication. In spite of the kindly treatment he was accorded, he evidently felt uprooted and homesick in the unfamiliar Northern surroundings. His teasing may have been misinterpreted. Whatever the reasons, he returned to Bavaria after one year. Now his widowed father decided to send him to a boarding school in Landshut, Bavaria.

Even in Hamburg the boy had enjoyed the sheltered atmosphere of a wealthy family circle; now he was exposed, all day long, to the impersonal life of an institution. In order to control the unruly hordes of youngsters, the teachers resorted to corporal punishment even for minor infractions of the rules. Christian felt humiliated, as he had never been punished in this fashion before. It was also inevitable that the sensitive and somewhat pampered boy should become a welcome target for the mischievous inclinations of some of his uncouth schoolmates. Morgenstern suffered emotionally more than physically. The boy complained bitterly in his letters to his father, who lent a sympathetic ear and consoled him with the promise of better days that were bound to come and unite them. Meanwhile he should realize that the greatness of outstanding men was often due to hardships they had encountered and overcome in their younger years. On March 30, 1884, two years after he had entered the boarding school, the boy was permitted to leave because his father had been appointed professor at the Royal Academy of Art in Breslau and had married Amélie von Dall'Armi. Christian joined them in Breslau, where he attended the Maria-Magdalena Gymnasium for four years.

In 1906, when reading the biography of Krapotkin, who had had the right kind of guidance during his formative years, Morgenstern became painfully aware of the contrast to his own life. He felt prompted to remark: "Almost all I have achieved I owe to my own efforts, to a few private individuals and to chance. I never felt part of any articulate, cohesive culture which the individual could have used for systematic education. Neither parents nor teachers nor anyone else molded me with a strong hand and educated me, in the higher sense of the word. And if I, originally a person of brilliant talents, by and large have remained an amateur, I must put the blame on the enormous amount of dilettantism, halfheartedness, and lack of culture that I encountered."[2] Such harsh words are rarely found in Morgenstern's writings. They testify to the high standards that he, a free-lance writer and poet, set for himself. They were written after the estrangement from his father and imply that the latter was unable or unwilling to provide the strong personal leadership that Christian subconsciously expected during his formative years. The passage is also an indictment of the secondary school where the young man did not find any teachers who really inspired him. In fact, after graduation, looking back over his high school years, he vented his feelings of disillusionment in a condemnatory appraisal of the German *Gymnasium*: "First, the school induced me to be insincere, then it endangered my moral standards, it caused embitterment and gloom by completely disregarding and ridiculing my individuality and, finally, it bored me to death. If, in spite of all this, I hope to become a tolerably rational person, it is due to my innate disposition, which is inclined to reflection, and above all, to all those who were fond and are fond of me, my parents and my friends."[3] Morgenstern recognized here two main factors in the development of his personality, his gift to attract others and communicate with them effectively, and his urge to devote himself to intellectual and spiritual matters.

At the *Gymnasium* in Breslau, the newcomer was soon recognized for his unpredictable mind and his poetic talent. Since he did not excel in the regular subjects, he admittedly dashed off poems to convince his classmates that he was not stupid but merely lazy. In his eagerness to create new sound effects, he invented a secret language for his intimate friends, a forerunner of some of the poems in the *Gallows Songs*. One of his extracurricular activities was the study of Volapük, a contrived universal language that preceded Esperanto. As he grew more mature, philosophy aroused his keenest interest. In his autobiographical summary, Morgenstern states that he experienced "the first thrill of philosophical discussions" at the age of sixteen (S, 11). He was fascinated by Schopenhauer's ideas and attracted by his masterful style. His first acquaintance with oriental metaphysics and with German mystics such as Angelus Silesius, Meister Eckhart, and Tauler probably came to him through Schopenhauer. Morgenstern never accepted Schopenhauer's pessimism or his splitting up of reality into a phenomenal world of illusion and an essential world behind it. Yet he felt stimulated by certain aspects of Schopenhauer's philosophy which awakened and strengthened kindred thoughts that had been dormant in him, such as the idea of reincarnation. In fact, reincarnation is the topic of one of his earliest poems printed posthumously and written when Morgenstern was only sixteen years old.

Just at the right time, a kind fate provided him with a kindred soul whose bearer was to become his best and lifelong friend—Friedrich Kayssler, the eminent actor. During the summer months of 1889 while his parents were traveling, Morgenstern stayed at a boardinghouse where Kayssler lived. He was eighteen, and his friend fifteen. They shared both boyish pranks and deep thoughts. Youthful enthusiasm united them, but in the fall Morgenstern left to attend a private officers' training school because his father, convinced that Christian did not have sufficient talent to become a painter, wanted him to enter a military career. However, it did not take long for the young man to realize that poetry, art, and the search for truth had become too much a part of his life. He promised his father that he would concentrate on his scholastic work, finish his studies at a *Gymnasium*, and enroll at a university.

The high school in the small town of Sorau (Lower Saxony) was chosen. Entering there in the spring of 1890, Morgenstern quickly earned the affection of his new classmates and inspired their confidence. He lived in the family of pastor Goettling, where he found a congenial atmosphere and an open-minded religious spirit that the young poet could respect and appreciate. The son, a classmate of his, became a good friend, and Marie Goettling, a few years older than he, took the place of a truly understanding, warm-hearted sister. With her Morgenstern exchanged letters until the end of his life. The spirit that pervaded the pastor's family strengthened Morgenstern's innate attitude toward his fellowmen. Half a year before graduating from high school he described it in a letter to Kayssler: "It is the feeling of an enormous duty to love, which everyone of us has toward his fellowmen and especially toward the suffering working class. I have acquired an understanding of the unheard-of, outrageous misery which surrounds us every hour—especially in the metropolis—and I have come to realize how despicable the behavior of all of us is, which ranges from contempt for the masses, lazy desire for a comfortable life, to lukewarm charity, without showing even a trace of true, active love, such as one brother should have for another." At the end of the letter, he speaks about his plans for the future: "I shall devote my whole life to this task, and if financial considerations should force me to give up the study of economics and political science, there will probably be other ways to practice and teach the gospel of *active* love" (*B*, October 7, 1891). Here we have Morgenstern's reason for choosing his field of study.

In the spring of 1892 he registered at the University of Breslau as a student of political science in the hope of becoming, some day, a promoter of social justice. Among his professors it was Felix Dahn, a well-known author of historical novels, who aroused his enthusiasm for the German nation and was indirectly responsible for Morgenstern's editing of the student magazine *Deutscher Geist*, which was circulated in mimeographed form. The continuation of his studies at the University of Munich in 1893 was destined to be short lived because the young student became seriously ill, and his tubercular condition, inherited from his mother, required an extensive period of recuperation in Silesia, first in Bad Reinerz and then in Nieder-Adelsbach near Salzbrunn. It was here that Morgenstern became acquainted with the peculiar humor of Laurence Sterne's *Tristram Shandy*. To his cousin Clara Ostler he wrote:

I am beside myself over the exceedingly glorious, grand book. Typically English in its rambling with its grotesque and ingenious notions it displays a humor and a most delicate irony that have a more exquisite bouquet than the finest Rhine wine. Time and again you see the author's face peep through the leaves, a maliciously obliging smile around his strangely twist-ing lips; at the same time, a thoroughly kind, dear face with flashing eyes and a high furrowed brow, a person who smilingly and tenderly looks down upon the small pieces of humanity and also upon himself, exclaiming: children, this is a funny world, and a foolish world, and a beautiful, glorious world. (*B*, July 21, 1893)

Morgenstern could appreciate this humor so thoroughly because it was an integral part of his own mental makeup. In these weeks he became fully aware of his poetic gifts. In a letter to Kayssler we find the passage: "For a change, my life appears to be more valuable than formerly. I have often told you of the stages I pass through. Well, my present stage, beginning with Reinerz (that is, Bad Reinerz in Silesia), has produced an ease of imagination and combinatory power that amazes me. As soon as I find a theme, its execution is effected with effortless speed. But how long will it last?" (*B*, August 19, 1893).

This last remark probably refers to his current period of creative productivity, but it could point also to his anticipated life span, because three weeks later he wrote to his cousin: "I have never been able to bring myself to believe that I would live to be fairly old, and although this conviction does not directly disturb me, it indirectly influences my thinking and striving since it confronts me continuously with the admonition: harvest as quickly as possible what you have to tell the world, before it is too late" (*B*, September 11, 1893). This sense of literary and poetic mission prompted him to devote most of his energy to creative writing and to make his facile pen the source of his support. Besides, this plan was dictated by necessity; for his father, who had married a third time after divorcing his second wife, was no longer willing to finance Christian's education, and he was too proud to permit his son to accept a gift from his young friends that would have provided a rest cure in Davos, Switzerland. However painful the ensuing estrangement between him and his father was for Christian, he later came to realize that complete independence was the best thing that could have happened to him. Since he could not go to Switzerland, the doctor advised him to live a very cautious and quiet life at home.

In the seclusion of his attic room he now became engrossed in Nietzsche's writings and thus experienced his first great intellectual encounter. In Morgenstern's *Stufen, eine Entwicklung in Aphorismen und Tagebuch-Notizen,* collected and edited by the poet's widow four years after his death, we find almost five pages devoted to Nietzsche. They show the poet's long-lasting and gradually changing reaction to the powerful challenge that Nietzsche meant to him. Summing up this influence in the last entry dated 1912, Morgenstern says: "Isn't Nietzsche one of our foremost stylists? And yet he remained sterile in a higher sense. I am weighing my words, for I have experienced Nietzsche if anyone ever has. And he was not sterile in me. But I also know in what respect he was my highest ideal for a long time: in his greatness as a human being, not in the overly modern type of his philosophy. This was dusk, not dawn, and whoever proceeds from there walks into—night" (S, 91). Already, six years earlier, Morgenstern had made the statement: "*Zarathustra,* with all its irrefutable greatness, is one of the worst books we have. It is neither a book for the ordinary reader nor a book for the finicky and lonely, it is a mixture of the grandiose and the banal in its contents as well as in its style" (S, 89).

CHAPTER 2

The Early Berlin Years

AFTER the secluded life in Breslau the young poet hoped to find stimulation and the proper atmosphere for creative work among the young artists and writers in the German capital. He took up residence there in the spring of 1894, and he was not disappointed. His letters express happiness over his creative mood. Living in a small attic room in the heart of Berlin near the castle and the art galleries, he felt in perfect health. Soon he was invited to send contributions to nine different journals and newspapers. He became a regular contributor of the *Neue Deutsche Rundschau,* charged with a quarterly review of contemporary lyrics. And the famous magazine *Der Kunstwart* commissioned him to write theater reviews in its Berlin supplement. At the same time, Morgenstern took full advantage of the many cultural opportunities which the metropolis offered him, notably concerts and plays. He became a member of the literary circle that gathered around Heinrich and Julius Hart. But more important than all these contacts was his friendship with Kayssler, who had stood by him in the dark Breslau days and who had now come to Berlin to become an actor.

Morgenstern deplored the materialistic tenor of contemporary culture. But he appreciated what Berlin could offer him: superb concerts and the vitality of the modern stage. A performance of Gerhart Hauptmann's *Florian Geyer* made a very deep impression on him, and the most famous producer of this time, Max Reinhardt, was among his friends. So we understand when he writes to Kayssler: "Berlin is the only air which I can still breathe, except great, eternal nature where I must be all by myself" (*B*, July 6, 1894). When, in view of the poet's precarious health, his friend suggested a more southern climate, Morgenstern answered: "I much prefer to stay in Berlin. If winter should give me any trouble I promise you that I will leave. It is never too late when I keep my condition in mind. To be sure, the financial situation is more difficult than you and I think. But no matter. I am only concerned with what every poet considers to be his mission. Only the weakling gives up. I don't expect much sympathy from my family any more. Their main concern is to have me stand on my own feet." In a subsequent passage of the same letter he says: "I am the only grandson of a wealthy grandfather, and as the only son of a well-paid state official I have been thrown out on the street pennyless, and after three bungled and dragged-out semesters I have been deprived of the possibility of finishing my studies. For where a person must spread himself so thin as I am doing here he cannot get anywhere in his study of the history of art. I simply cannot serve several masters" (B, fall, 1894). The reason why Morgenstern thought of changing his field of academic study was the fact that his father had procured for him a part-time job at the National Gallery. But the compensation was so small and the work so time-consuming that the poet gave it up after a few months. From now on his literary work was his only means of subsistence.

In Phanta's Schloss (In Fancy's Castle) is the title of Morgenstern's first volume of poetry. Written in two attic rooms, one in Breslau, the other in Berlin, its chief inspiration was Nietzsche. This is clearly expressed in the letter which the poet sent to Nietzsche's mother along with a copy of his book. Here he says: "I, a young man of twenty-four, dare to place my first poetic work into the hands of *the* mother, the venerable mother who has given such a great son to the world and to me especially a liberator, one who set an example for me and inspired me to the loftiest struggles of life. That spirit of victorious, proud transfiguration of life, that feeling of sovereign domination over all things, of which the beloved lonely man has spoken so often, also pervades, I believe, these poems submitted to you, the greater part of which I dare to call humorous in the most subtle sense of the word" (B, May 6, 1895). Here is the key to the understanding of *In Phanta's Schloss*, which its author characterizes as humorous and fantastic. Mythological, cosmic, and middle-class concepts surprise us here in their striking combination.

The rising moon is a glistening soap bubble which Pan, lying in the bushes surrounding the pond, has blown into the air with a reed. Now he gazes at the fragile ball as it is carried aloft by the wind. The hymns of Klopstock and young Goethe come to mind when we read "Sunrise," a serious poem in which Morgenstern expresses his lofty emotions as he witnesses a sunrise in the mountains:

> In den Ätherwellen des Alls
> bewusst mitschwingen,
> eins mit der Ewigkeit,
> leibvergessen, zeitlos
> in sich der Ewigkeit
> flutende Akkorde—

To vibrate consciously with the ethereal waves of the universe, one with eternity, oblivious of one's body, timeless, the undulating chords of eternity within.

Here Morgenstern anticipates feelings that he was to put into verse in some of his very last lyrics. One of the best poems in this collection is called "Auffahrt" ("Ascent"). The relentless drive to the stars in the phantom chariot drawn by steeds of the night is described in effectively changing rhythm and a varied rhyme scheme. The sound of a distant waterfall is the last vanishing impression from the earth before the poet enters the deep solitude of his dream world that may reveal to him the mysteries of the universe. *In Phanta's Schloss* was well received, especially by the young literary set in Berlin. Rilke was greatly impressed and described his reaction in verse on the flyleaf of his copy.

To some of his readers Morgenstern's humor must have sounded like irony. But he assures them: "Don't let yourselves be misled by my irony. My irony is as unsophisticated as my pathos. I can say incredible things ironically without a trace of frivolity; yes, perhaps, I wrote them with a serious face without any laughter other than that of an unruffled, serene mind" (S, 15). This serenity stems from Morgenstern's deep-seated love for all the world. He was convinced that "the more you love the world the more beautiful it will appear to you" (S, 151). This is the basis from which the artist should proceed. Of his goal Morgenstern remarks: "A spiritualization of reality at every point . . . an artistic politheism (from an artist's point of view)—this, I feel, must be the program for the future. The victory of the human mind over matter must be complete" (S, 57). If we keep in mind that these words were written in 1895, that is, in the heyday of photographic realism in German literature, we can imagine Morgenstern's position among the intellectuals of those days. He saw the contemporary literary movement in perspective and wrote in 1896: "The naturalistic drama is of value only if it makes man, such as he is today, disgusted with himself. Ibsen, Hauptmann, literary realism constitute an historical phase in the artist's approach. Naturalism is merely an epoch, not a goal" (S, 58).

Serenity was a state of mind ardently wished for but not always attained by Morgenstern. Thus in 1897 he wrote: "There is hardly a greater disillusionment than when you come to indifferent people with a really great joy in your heart" (S, 177). A few months earlier, he had confessed to the editor of a journal who wanted a review of the works of contemporary writers: "I see very little culture in all the activity whose chief characteristic is an enormous conceit" (B, September 28, 1896). On the other hand, the poet was not immune to the admiration of some young people of the gentler sex, and many could not help being attracted to him. But he was very solicitous about his personal freedom. One of his more personal poems begins with the words: "Ich bin ein Mensch von echter Vogel-Art" ("I am very birdlike kind of man") and goes on to say: "And I don't like to be clasped in anyone's arms. The happiness of unimpeded wandering will always move my heart most joyfully." The poem ends: "And even if I feel a gentle longing, from the luring call of many a belle, no charmer has been able yet to get me permanently accustomed to her domain." The humor and vivacity of young Morgenstern made him a welcome guest in many artistic circles. In a letter to Marie Goettling he admits: "Berlin has again caught me in its claws. So I have already decided to intersperse a hermit's week. There is one good friend after another whose chummy evenings I am supposed to attend, and in a jiffy a person is turned from a worker into a parasite" (B, January 24, 1897).

Already in the first weeks he spent in Berlin Morgenstern discovered nature. He was enthusiastic about the Tiergarten, "but the dearest spot in Berlin is for me the chestnut grove near the university." One of his best-known early lyrics was composed in 1894; it is entitled "Frühling" ("Spring").

> Wie ein Geliebter seines Mädchens Kopf,
> den süssen Kopf mit seiner Welt voll Glück,
> in seine beiden armen Hände nimmt,
> so fass ich deinen Frühlingskopf, Natur,
> dein überschwänglich holdes Maienhaupt,
> in meine armen, schlichten Menschenhände,
> indes du lächelnd mir ins Auge schaust,
> und stammle leis dir das Bekenntnis zu:
> Vor so viel Schönheit schweigt mein tiefstes Lied.

Just as a lover takes the head of his beloved, the sweet head with its world full of happiness, into his two poor hands, thus I take your vernal head, nature, your rapturously charming head in May, into my poor, plain human hands and, deeply moved, I silently immerse myself in you while you look smilingly into my eyes and softly make my stammering confession unto you: confronted with so much beauty, my deepest song grows mute.

Although this poem was immediately accepted by the literary magazine *Die Freie Bühne*, later called *Die Neue Rundschau*, it does not appear in the collection *Auf vielen Wegen (On Many Roads)* which was published in 1897 and subsequently enlarged and combined with another thin volume of lyrics called *Ich und die Welt (I and the World)*. As the original title indicates, the collection offers a large variety of themes, moods, and lyric forms. These lyrics range from a lighthearted song of sheer joy in life, written in unconventional stanzas, to the meditative free verse groping for the meaning of human existence. Frequently the earthbound and spiritual are contrasted, as in the poem "Inmitten der grossen Stadt" ("In the Midst of the Large City"). Here we see the silent river flowing through the metropolis at night, reflecting the thousands of stars above while man is lost in fleeting moments of pleasure and pain, unaware of himself as part of the universe. "Morgenfahrt" ("Morning Ride") describes a sunrise impressionistically in three four-line rhymed stanzas. This is quite different from the dithyrambic effusion of *In Phanta's Schloss* which Morgenstern composed in the same period. The poet rides across the countryside at night through the silent fields and black woods until, at last, streaks of yellow and rose appear on the distant horizon. A fiery ball emerges from the damp fog and sheds its purple glow over the fields, transforming the woods into a billowy sea of gold. A flash of light penetrates the twilight of the coach, kissing the poet's soul from its sleep and fortifying him for battle: "Ein Flammengruss aus der Unendlichkeit" ("A flaming salute from infinity").

Morgenstern demonstrates his early mastery of lyrical rhythm and alliteration in the poem "Auf dem Strome":

> Eine Welle läuft leise
> schon lang nebenher,
> sie denkt wohl, ich reise
> hinunter zum Meer

A wave has been hurrying softly alongside of me. It probably thinks I am traveling down to the sea.

These lines are taken from the second of three long stanzas that describe a boat ride at night from the chilling evening breeze to the uncertain goal at dawn, as the poet drifts on and on. "An die Wolken" ("To the Clouds") is an unrhymed hymn in free verse. It expresses the poet's longing to get away from the confining life and folly of society, to be free like the clouds, these eternal thoughts of heaven, which he follows with his eyes as they sail across land and sea over the abyss of boundless space and vanishing, in the end, before the myriads of stars shining over unfathomable depths.

Morgenstern's mythologizing imagination creates gods that live in the azure above the clouds like shepherds in the Elysian fields sending their roaring laughter to the gods on other stars. They know very little about all the tiny creatures below. But why should we shed empty tears: "We are gods, too, you and I." This seems to be spoken in a tone of good-humored jest and ends the three rhymed stanzas entitled "Wohl kreist verdunkelt oft der Ball" ("The Globe

May Often Rotate in Darkness"). In a terrestial counterpart, Morgenstern describes those happy human beings who are children of fortune. They throw glistening balls and light up the faces of those whom they meet. A woman's soft arms embrace them, and the air is scented with their sweet kisses. Their words are melodious, and laughingly they hurl sonorous flashes of lightning at their attacking foes. Their quick resolve forestalls the plans of their worst enemies. With innocent minds they reap what others sowed laboriously. This lively poem, with its quick rhythm, called "Die Kinder des Glücks" ("The Children of Fortune") repeats in the last stanza the words of the first one:

> Sorglosen Lächelns
> die Lippen geschürzt
> fröhlich die blühenden
> Wangen gerötet,
> tanzen wir Kinder des Glücks
> unsre sonnigen Pfade dahin.

With carefree smile, our lips pursed, our blooming cheeks flushed with joy, we children of fortune dance along on our sunny paths.

Morgenstern's charming humor—not the grotesque humor of the *Galgenlieder* but the kind we encounter in Gottfried Keller—is also represented in the collection *Auf vielen Wegen*. There is the "Kleine Geschichte" ("Little Story") of the little flag that was in great distress because its red and yellow stripes wanted to unite. It billowed and waved and flicked but could not cross the segregating seams:

> Da kam ein Wolkenbruch daher
> und wusch das Fähnlein kreuz und quer
> dass Rot und Gelb, zerflossen
> voll Inbrunst sich genossen.

Then a cloudburst came up and drenched the little flag up and down and back and forth, so that red and yellow, fused, most ardently enjoyed each other.

The last stanza says: "The owners of the flag, to be sure, could not understand the joyfulness of the event, while those who were united forgot the rest of the world." The simple language of the folk song is apparent, just as it is in the other tale called "Anmutiger Vertrag" ("Charming Pact"), where the poet and the nightingale come to a charming agreement. We are reminded of a similar situation in Walther von der Vogelweide of whose lyrics Morgenstern compiled a small anthology in 1906. Yesterday—the poet relates—two people kissed each other on the bench in the woods. Today the nightingale came and fetched what was left. When parting, the girl had put up her braids again; how much blonde silk that nightingale found there. With its beak filled with gossamer the nightingale returned home and lined the fragile nest with its gold. Friend nightingale, the poet exclaims at the end, let it be thus every year: for me your song and for you a few strands of my beloved's hair.

In the winter months of 1896–1897 Morgenstern had a number of significant dreams which he fashioned into a cycle of twelve lyrics forming part of *Auf vielen Wegen*. The best known of these is entitled "Der Stern" ("The Star"), symbolizing the poet's higher world. Just as daytime experiences are usually more concise and more sharply delineated than the imagined happenings of our dreams, Morgenstern's description of his dream is more extended than his portrayal of the physical world; it is presented in free verse in long unrhymed lines and slow rhythm. The poet saw himself as a pale boy stretched out asleep in a canoe while the mysterious celestial gleam penetrated the delicate web of his eyelids. His entire inner being became luminous with the enchantment of a higher world. A soft ringing held him spellbound as if the ray of every star conveyed a tone from a distant homeland. He was haunted by a sweet song that gradually silenced all other sounds. The song came from departed souls promising him a richer existence endowed with higher faculties. They lured him to happier spheres free from suffering and earthly limitations where beauty reigns and unselfish love, where there is no sin and no guilt. The sound of a ponderous bell interrupted the clear, pure voices of the other world. The poet half raised himself up from his bed, saw through the open window many stars sparkling—and dropped back to sleep. This longing for the serenity and purity of a higher world, his spiritual home, expressed in this dream is found also in the description of a creative hour written a year earlier. In his creative moment Morgenstern feels at one with the universe; he senses the breath of eternity, and the rhythm of the worlds is in him. All stars send delicate vibrations to him, and he responds secretly in soft waves. His happiness is imparted to the ether, which is vibrant with his song.

While Morgenstern experienced his individuality as part of the universe in cosmic dimensions, he viewed his present life on earth as one incarnation preceded by others. Even as a sixteen-year-old boy he wrote a poem on reincarnation. Speaking of death as a liberator of man, Morgenstern says that, even if he should rise again and live on earth and strive and pass away, he will progress through the changes of time to attain maturity and life in eternity (*M,* 7). Five years later, the poet speaks of his reassuring conviction that he will never die, that he will accomplish his work even though his body may be destroyed, that he will rebound from that failure of his plans because he knows that what he is doing and that to which he is aspiring is not confined to the span of *one* life (*M,* 16). We find the culmination of this trend of thought expressed in two poems from *Mensch Wanderer* in the two stanzas entitled "Künstler-Ideal" included in *Auf vielen Wegen.* The poem begins:

> O tiefe Sehnsucht, die ich habe
> erfülltest du dich einst einmal,
> dass ich nach dieses Lebens Grabe
> mich wiederfänd in Lust und Qual—
> in einem neuen Künstlerwerden,
> in einem Gott des Tons, des Steins . . .
> dass ich in ewigen Gerberden
> so webte am Gewand des Scheins.

Oh deep longing that I feel, if only you should be fulfilled some day, that I should find myself after this life's grave in joy and sorrow—in an artist's new existence, in a God of music and sculpture so that I could weave in unending motions at the garment of the phenomenal world.

The second stanza is a variation of the same theme: even though anguish and sorrow may be the artist's lot, to be a creator seems to be the only worthy goal. Oh, to rise again and again with full hands, a master of beauty, to go from world to world, an unknown god with lofty torches.

Following the cycle of twelve dreams we find, in *Auf vielen Wegen,* some kind of Dance of Death, a sequence of poems under the caption "Vom Tagewerk des Todes" ("On the Labor of Death"). Death appears in the guise of the sower who in sowing wastes innumerable seeds, as the guest who turns into the solitary toper, as the reaper who comes to the blacksmith, as the ghostly pilot causing the boat to be shipwrecked, as the drunken switchman on the last trip, as the stranger who pushes the mountain climber into the abyss and, finally, as the visitor coming to the sick man in his delirious dream. Better known than these episodes in verse is the poem entitled "Vöglein Schwermut" ("The Little Bird Melancholy") which belongs to the same group. The imaginary bird called melancholy flies across the world singing such a mournful song that anyone who hears it cannot hear anything else. He can no longer endure the light of day and does away with himself. Every midnight the bird takes its rest on the finger of death. He strokes it softly and says; "fly away, my little bird, fly away." And again it flies across the world singing. In its language this poem approaches the manner of the folk song. Its form is light-winged in spite of the deadly seriousness of its contents.

The vitality of Morgenstern's mind in those years is seen in the variety of poetic projects and unfinished plans. Thus he created a humorous counterpart to the odes of Horace with a setting in modern Berlin. They were published in the spring of 1896 under the title *Horatius Travestitus.* The little book was so successful that a second edition became necessary the following year. In 1911 Reinhard Piper, the poet's publisher, urged Morgenstern to expand the small collection. A few odes were added with the introductory remark: "The translator succeeded in locating the manuscript of a fifth book of odes by Horace in a small unknown town in Italy." In one of these added odes Morgenstern relates that he saw the last god who had resided in Tibur leaving the place and approaching him with the request to offer him shelter for the last night. He had suffered for a long time, first in Rome, then in Tibur when Rome had become hell to him. But Tibur, too, was overrun with traffic. The mad people painted a stop sign on his little temple. There was a hustle and bustle, day and night, and no man and no god could get a chance to sleep and rest. So he started out for Germany. The last stanza reads:

> Und so zog er beim Morgengraun
> Wirklich fort in dies Land, wo, wie er sagte, die
> Menschen Dichter und Denker sind:
> und so zog er denn, traun! fort nach—Utopia.

And thus he started out at the crack of dawn, leaving for this country where, as he said, the people are poets and thinkers: and thus he started out, forsooth, for Utopia.

In August, 1895, Morgenstern traveled to the island of Sylt in the North Sea. The sight of the ocean was an overpowering experience. The world of music, especially Beethoven's symphonies which he had heard in Berlin, came to life as he watched the waves surging toward him. Here the poet conceived a great lyrical work appropriately called *Symphonie*. It was to express his concern about all things temporal and eternal. This verbal piece of music was to consist of four movements. In the first movement "the descent to hell, to the dregs of society" was to be presented. In contrast, the second movement (an adagio) was to convey serene peace. The third movement (a scherzo) was to find its climax in a children's dance, while the fourth was to include a prayer for rebirth and rousing hymns addressed to the artists and to Germany. Morgenstern never succeeded in carrying out his grandiose design. Even more grandiose was the grotesque thought expressed by the poet that our world was merely the product of the prodigious imagination of a mischievous deity. The playful supraterrestial view point of "Welt-Kobold" ("World Goblin") must have appealed to Morgenstern, although he did not get beyond a few sketchy scenes in verse.

CHAPTER 3

The Early Years Abroad

H ENRIK Ibsen, the Norwegian playwright, was at the zenith of his fame when his collected works appeared in German, published by S. Fischer, who also brought out Morgenstern's latest lyrics. Already as a high school student the latter had been acquainted with Ibsen's social dramas. Although he had strong reservations about them, he now felt quite honored when he was asked to become the official translator of Ibsen's plays in verse. He accepted the offer, fully aware of how difficult a task it would be, especially since he had no knowledge of the Norwegian tongue. He realized that he would have to give this assignment priority over his own poetic plans. Only in this manner did he succeed in meeting the deadline for his translation of the *Festival at Solhaug* in February, 1898. In May of that year he traveled to Norway to acquire a firsthand knowledge of the setting of Ibsen's plays and, possibly, to meet the playwright himself.

He found very satisfactory accommodations in a sanitarium in Nordstrand, not far from Kristiania (Oslo). In a letter to Marie Goettling, Morgenstern describes the view from his window across the brook over the fjord. He speaks of the ever-changing attractions of this beautiful landscape: "Now there is heavy snow everywhere. Everything is like a large silver platter embossed and engraved . . . then the sunsets and the moonlit nights. I can think only with sadness of the fact that some day I shall have to leave here. The air is the very essence of health; the cold in spite of the low temperature, is not unpleasant because there is no wind; the people, in all their calmness and soundness, their natural cheerfulness, fit in beautifully" (*B*, January 20, 1899). In the same letter he talks about his activities: "About three times a week I take a fifteen-minute ride by rail to the city. There I go to the University Library, the Art Museum, the theater, or the concert, or I am invited to visit friends. Often I go to the harbor, an eager observer, happily immersed in mere watching. I tell you, the painter in me is, as always, my real soul. Sometimes I am almost submerged in the innumerable influences of nature upon me." This closer contact with nature could not help but be reflected in Morgenstern's poetry. At the same time, his intensive occupation with Ibsen's dramatic language was not without influence on his own shorter poems and his epigrams.

Friendly relations were soon established between the playwright and his translator. Ibsen had high praise for the translation and called the scenes from *"Brand"* which Morgenstern had sent him a splendid piece of work. The translation of Ibsen's *Comedy of Love* was generally recognized in its excellence. As E. Brausewetter has pointed out, Morgenstern succeeded in solving the difficult task of translating Ibsen's verses, which were fraught with ideas, images, and ingenious puns, without any loss. In fact, Ibsen had so much confidence in Morgenstern's art of translating that he asked him personally to go over the text of other translated works. This assignment cost Morgenstern a great deal of time and effort. Even before Ibsen finished his last drama *When We Dead Awaken*, he expressed the wish that Morgenstern should take over the German translation. Upon his return to Berlin in the fall of 1899, Morgenstern tackled the task together with Elias, the editor of Ibsen's completed works in German, and completed it by Christmas.

The two plays that offered a special challenge to Morgenstern were *Brand* and *Peer Gynt*. The former interested him in its unconventional modern religious outlook, while the latter appealed to him, in its grotesque aspects, as a caricature of middle-class complacency. In the fourth act of *Peer Gynt* we believe we can hear an echo of Morgenstern's humorous creation, Palmström. Interrupted by the translator's frequent travels and rest cures necessitated by his physical condition, the translation dragged on and sometimes appeared as a burdensome task that impeded Morgenstern's creative work. In the end, he was especially anxious to finish the translation of Ibsen's poems because they were somewhat alien to him. But the standard of translation was uniformly high, and after the master's death in 1906 his widow sent a silver medallion along with flowers from his coffin to six personalities who had been most helpful in promoting her late husband's work. Morgenstern was one of them. Ibsen's fame was largely based on the up-to-dateness of the social problems of his day that he presented with great dramatic skill. It has, therefore, lost some of its luster. As a translator of some of Ibsen's works Morgenstern has been practically forgotten, while his own poetry, especially his humorous poems, which he created in those years and shortly afterward, are alive and appreciated as much as ever.

In August, 1898, Morgenstern wrote from Nordstrand: "My next collection of songs will be an intermezzo, a piece of blue sky. It dates from this spring and summer and certainly is the simplest of all my lyrics so far" (B, August 26, 1898). The poet now tried to make this earth his home. He wanted to be happy in order to be able to make others happy. He called the collection *Ein Sommer (A Summer)* and dedicated it to Dagny Fett, his youthful friend. Its poems appear almost exactly in the order in which they were composed. They reflect a great joy in color and, at the same time, reveal a great tenderness and delicacy of feeling. Dagny's family, viewing Morgenstern's tender, somewhat fatherly concern for the young girl, expected a firmer, more conventional commitment on the part of the poet; this he could not make. He pleaded with Dagny:

> Ich bin ein Rohr im Wind
> Bind nicht an mich dein Boot,
> es wär für dich, lieb Kind
> wie mich—der Tod.[1]

I am a reed in the wind. Don't moor your boat to me; it would mean death for you, dear child, and death for me.

In the summer of 1899 Morgenstern left Oslo for the northern regions of Norway, the setting of *Brand* and *Peer Gynt*. He traveled along the coast as far as Molde. Here he was enchanted by the deep blue of the fjords encircled by snow-covered mountains and long rocky islands. He saw nature in its immaculate majesty. A medical examination in Bergen brought home to him again the seriousness of his tubercular condition. The poet's momentary mood is expressed in these lines:

> Dunkler Tropfe,
> der mir heut in den Becher fiel
> in den Becher des Lebens,
> dunkler Tropfe Tod.[2]

Dark drop that fell into my cup today, into the cup of life, dark drop of death.

From now on he had to live more cautiously. He returned to Berlin in the fall of 1899, but less than a year later he was compelled to seek the thinner, purer air of Davos, Switzerland. He had found the conditions in the German capital depressing after his return from Norway. His humor proved to be a necessary weapon for self-assertion. Morgenstern parodied the then popular family drama in his dramatic sketch *Egon und Emilie*, where the hero is dragged upon the stage. All attempts of his girl friend to engage him in suitable conversation which would give rise to a family tragedy are of no avail. He persists in being silent. Finally, the curtain falls, the audience disbands. There will be no family tragedy this time.

Another dramatic sketch called *Das Mahl (The Meal)* is a parody of a play by D'Annunzio. The soup is finally served, but the young boy, who is famished, is not allowed to start eating because his father continues entertaining his guests with an enthusiastic description of a sumptuous, elaborate meal in ancient times. When he finally finds his way back to reality, the soup is no longer hot and is sent back to the kitchen. In the end, the boy faints from hunger and everybody gets upset on account of the would-be aesthete who, in his poetic effusions, forgets the common human needs at hand. Ernst von Wolzogen, whose recently established literary vaudeville called *Überbrettl* specialized in satirizing the fads and foibles of the day, was delighted to present this and other dramatic sketches by Morgenstern, and did so with great success.

Meanwhile the poet had become a patient at the sanitarium of Dr. Turban in Davos, Switzerland. We know from Thomas Mann's novel *Der Zauberberg (The Magic Mountain)* how hard these health establishments tried to occupy the enforced leisure time of their patients by a rigorously imposed daily routine. Some seventy other patients were governed by the same regulations. Morgenstern complained about the lack of privacy—which he needed for his creative work. Although his present condition was medically satisfactory, he was troubled about what the future would hold for him and his art. He was reading Nietzsche's letters and again was greatly impressed by his genius. Next to Nietzsche he considered Paul de Lagarde as the leading German of the last two decades. It is ironic that one of Morgenstern's Jewish friends and admirers, Efraim Frisch in Berlin, attracted the poet's attention to this Old Testament scholar who had become the defender of an anti-Semitic pan-Germanism. To be sure, what impressed Morgenstern so strongly were not so much Lagarde's political views or his anti-Semitic bias but the vision of *Die Religion der Zukunft (The Religion of the Future)*, as he called his book, which was published in 1878. Here he emphasized a personal, mystical relationship to God which was the result of a spiritual rebirth of the individual. God's indwelling in the soul of man, as presented by Lagarde, was an essential ingredient in Morgenstern's monistic mysticism which found its fullest expression in *Tagebuch eines Mystikers* (1906). Under the impact of Lagarde's writings Morgenstern began to read the Old and the New Testament. He felt that a new culture must be based on a new religious experience which, in turn, would create a new community among men.

We know from a letter which Morgenstern wrote to his stepmother on New Year's Eve, 1901, that he would have preferred to go to Rome and Florence to do research for a drama on Savonarola, but that he had to finish the translation of Ibsen's poems. He also realized how beneficial the high mountains had been for his lungs the previous winter. So he chose Arosa, which is located still higher than Davos and could then be reached only by mailcoach. Here he had the time for intensive reading. Besides studying Lagarde and Tolstoy, he read the posthumously published notes for Nietzsche's unfinished principal work *Der Wille Zur Macht (The Will to Power)*. Morgenstern wrote to Frisch about these plans: "They are for me the most powerful revelation of the human spirit that I know. I don't believe that any human being ever had a deeper insight than the Nietzsche of this book. Even the rest of his work vanishes for me when compared with this last legacy that he wrote down on the eve of his spiritual death with a vigor and clarity for which we can only feel a silent reverence" (*B*, Februray 24, 1902).

Morgenstern's Italian journey was carried out the following spring. The poet traveled from Zurich to Milan, Rapallo, and on to Portofino. In Florence he stayed for two weeks, deeply impressed by the art treasures there. He started out on his return trip on Whitsunday. The five hours he had between trains in Milan were used for a visit to the famous cathedral. As Morgenstern reported later:

This was a church that could, in its own way, come up to what we think a Greek temple must have meant. This, people will say, was the great Christian era on earth. . . . There is so much talk about art taking the place of religion. But art became homeless when there were no longer any religious structures where it could live, which it could fill with its soul, in which it could make its highest revelations accessible to everyone without exception. . . . We shall have culture when this nation, no longer satisfied with a purely personal art, starts out to seek a higher expression of its ardent desire to put its life on a higher plane, when it will venture to build the first edifice in which to express its new soul. This ideal structure could mean the beginning of our culture. In it the highest achievements of our painters and sculptors will have their home."[3]

In his ardent desire to help bring about a new culture, Morgenstern sometimes regretted that his artistic ability was confined to producing poetry, that he was no universal genius. For a colorful landscape he could find only words. He felt that no one could see the world as he did, no one could penetrate with such joyful senses the mysteries of nature and experience such gratitude of the human soul toward all life as he did (*M*, 57). Sometimes Morgenstern wondered what he was doing in a strange country, among strange people. He felt like a huge eye that gazes in innocent happiness and amazement at a universe it cannot comprehend (*M*, 49). One day the poet was standing in the doorway of a house, engaged in conversation with the people inside, when from the outside he heard an

Aeolian harp. Then the symbolic significance of his present situation
dawned on him and almost moved him to tears. He was part of the
workaday-world, but one ear would always be tuned to the melody
of the everlasting generative forces of life (M, 54). A few of
Morgenstern's poems of those years deal with the creative process.
In one of these, he likens the heavenly bliss of the creative moment
to the enchantment of the anointed walking over the waves and of
the gods above the clouds who created the world. We also have the
actual description of the genesis of a poem that was the product of
the momentary atmosphere created by its setting:

> Ihr müsst solche Verse nicht anders betrachten
> als wie sie Zeit und Umstände brachten.
> Schenkte der Tag sein redliches Werk,
> so lag ich ein Stück in dem Wald, auf dem Berg,
> und wie ein Falter vorüberfliegt
> und eine Erdbeere im Grünen liegt,
> so kam eine Stimmung, so bot sich ein Reim,
> und Falter und Erdbeere mussten mit heim.
>
> (M, 57)

You must consider such verse just as time and circumstances offered them
to me. When I was granted an honest day's work and was lying for a while in
the forest or on the mountain, and as a butterfly was flitting by and a
strawberry was lying in the grass the right mood came over me and I found a
rhyme, thus the butterfly and the strawberry had to come home with me.

The work of art is like a precious fruit that ripens in the artist's soul.
Seized with ecstasy in its autumnal ripeness, it overflows and spends
its very essence creating happiness in others (M, 59). Morgenstern
was aware that in fulfilling himself he was fulfilling his poetic mis-
sion; that was his lofty task and his destiny. In this sense he could
find his calling expressed in his own name: morning star. Addressing
his brothers-in-arms, he felt called upon to shine upon their banners
and lead them from darkness to the dawn of a new day (M, 55). In
his sacred mission he felt united in a vast league of kindred spirits:

> Eines Bunds geheime Glieder
> finden wir uns allerwärts:

und ich schenk Euch meine Lieder
und Ihr schenkt mir Euer Herz.

(M, 64)

We find each other everywhere as secret members of one league, and I give you my songs and you give me your hearts.

At the very beginning of this century, when Morgenstern had to seek refuge in the Swiss Alps because of the treacherous disease of his lungs, he had enough opportunity to ponder his fate as a human being. On one of his solitary walks he spotted a wooden hut near a steep rocky wall. It was surrounded by boulders that seemed to have plunged from the high rocks. In his poetic mind, this scene became an image of the frailty of human existence in the grips of an overhanging fate (*M*, 73). As to his personal fate, it could not help but deeply disturb the poet at times. When he watched a canoe one night chained to a post rocked by the waves, tugging and jerking and groaning for hours, as if it were straining to be released, he felt the chain that tied him to his fate (*M*, 85). Morgenstern's fate was a life in anticipation of an early death. What he feared more than the imminent end of his physical existence was spiritual extinction. At that time, he had no religious conviction in the traditional sense, but only an unfailing presentiment that his spiritual self in some way would outlast his earthly life. We find it expressed in his poem "Unverlierbare Gewähr" ("Unbreakable Guarantee"): "There is one thing that I can look forward to. It will not deceive me. Some evening, this heart will certainly rest from all its flights. This wanderer will then be allowed to sleep. He will have completed his work. What will continue to be awake will be something else, some other being" (*M*, 85). In the collected works which Piper published in one volume in 1965 this poem is followed by one composed in 1902 in the style of a folk song. It is a defiant battle song. The two poems present two facets of the same theme: the triumph of the human spirit over matter:

Es kommt der Schmerz gegangen
und streicht mir über die Wangen
wie seinem liebsten Kind.

Da tönt mein' Stimm' gebrochen
Doch meines Herzens Pochen
verzagt nicht so geschwind.

Und gäb die böse Stunde
noch gerner von sich Kunde:
mein Herz ist fromm und fest.
Ich bin ein guter Helde:
mein Lachen zieht zu Felde,
und Siegen ist der Rest.

(*M*, 81)

Pain is coming, stroking my cheeks, as if I were his dearest child. Then my voice is breaking. But my throbbing heart does not despair so quickly. And even if the evil hour would like to make itself felt still more: my heart is firm and steadfast. I am a good soldier; my laughter will fight for me, and what is left is victory.

It is strange that this laughter of Morgenstern's, his humor, has made him famous and has endeared him to thousands of readers who had no idea that it was his secret weapon in his struggle for life. The poet was well aware of his perilous condition, for in the same year he composed a poem entitled "Sei bereit" ("Be Ready") whose last stanza reads:

Und wie sich die Fackeln neigen
draussen zu des Tags Geleit,
fühl ich auch auf mich sie zeigen
und mir winken: sei bereit.
Wenn die Abendschatten steigen. . . .

(*M*, 88)

And as the torches are lowered outside to escort the day, I feel that they are pointing at me and beckon to me: be ready. When the shadows of the evening grow longer. . . .

In one of his darkest hours, he derived consolation from the thought that the rays from one special star were sent to him above all others to comfort him, assuring him that it was his good star and that he should leave all grief behind. The poem describing this experience begins with the words: "Es gibt noch Wunder, liebes Herz" ("Miracles still happen, dear heart").

Concluding this chapter, which covers the time from Morgenstern's departure for Norway in 1898 to his return to Berlin in May, 1903, I quote one of his best known shorter lyrics, composed probably in memory of Dagny and published in the collection *Ein Kranz* (*A Wreath*):

> Erster Schnee
> Aus silbergrauen Gründen tritt
> ein schlankes Reh
> im winterlichen Wald
> und prüft vorsichtig, Schritt für Schritt,
> den reinen, kühlen, frischgefallnen Schnee.
>
> Und Deiner denk ich, zierliche Gestalt.

First Snow: Out of the silvery gray distance steps a slender doe in the wintry woods and probes cautiously, step by step, the pure, cool, newly fallen snow. Of you I think, daintiest of all figures.

CHAPTER 4

Grotesque Humor

Galgenlieder *and* Palmström

A NY living creature has latent powers that are mobilized in the face of mortal danger. Man has, among other hidden resources, something that no animal can resort to, that is, a sense of humor which may come to his rescue by lifting his spirits in a desperate situation. If a person about to be hanged asserts his inner freedom by cracking jokes he displays what the Germans call *Galgenhumor* ("gallows humor").[1]

On one occasion, during his early Berlin years, Morgenstern joined his carefree friends on an outing to Werder near Potsdam. When they passed a hill called Galgenberg, the high-spirited group hit upon the idea of founding a "Club of the Gallows Gang." In organizing their spooky gatherings, they went to great lengths as they collected a variety of gruesome paraphernalia. The statutes were written on parchment spattered with blood-red ink stains. They called their hangout the *Stätte* ("place of execution"), and the waiter was called the *Knacker* ("executioner"). When they clinked glasses, they shouted "hang them." They created an appropriate environment, shrouding the lamp in a black veil and covering the table with a black cloth. On this table they placed the victim's last meal: bread and a cup of water. The following items were arranged on the table: a burning candle, a Bible with a rusty sword on top of it, a ball of red wool representing the thread of life, an hourglass, and a little bell to toll the knell. Morgenstern, the guiding spirit, would bring to the meetings a few new gallows songs scribbled on scraps of paper. Julius Hirschfeld, the composer, would try out an appropriate melody on the piano, and then the gallows gang would sing their songs together. Thus initially this grotesque poetry was

44

not meant at all for a reading public. The gallows songs were originally created for the entertainment of a small group of gleeful friends who were witty and unconventional enough to appreciate Morgenstern's fantastic creations.

Occasionally a few guests would be invited to this inner circle. Thus Morgenstern's buffoonery in verse became known among congenial young spirits. Ernst von Wolzogen soon presented *Galgenlieder* with considerable success in his literary vaudeville shows. Morgenstern continued to expand his collection of grotesque poems by inventing weird events and fabulous animals that were no longer directly connected with the gallows hill. When he finally decided to make these poems accessible to a wider circle of kindred spirits, he could not find a publisher courageous enough to take the risk of such an unconventional venture. Not until 1905 did Bruno Cassirer publish the slender volume called *Galgenlieder*, which became enormously popular during the poet's lifetime, and even more so after his death. One hundred thousand copies were sold within a quarter of a century and twice that many in an expanded edition called *Alle Galgenlieder* within five years of its 1932 publication.

Some critics, to be sure, did not appreciate that type of poetry and accused the poet of a lack of taste. Others were mystified and insisted on searching for a hidden key that would reveal the object of satire. And yet Morgenstern had dedicated these *Galgenlieder* "to the child in man," referring to Nietzsche's statement: "In any genuine man a child is hidden who wants to play." In the fifteenth edition of 1913 the poet added this explanation:

A child is hidden in every genuine human being, that is, a creative instinct, and for his dearest plaything or real thing he does not want the miniature boat that is a true imitation to the nth degree, but the shell of a walnut with a bird's feather as its mast and a pebble as its captain. This child wants the opportunity to be part of the play, of the creative act, and not so much to be merely an admiring spectator. For this child in the human being is the everlasting creative power in him.

In his "Attempt at an Introduction," Morgenstern could not resist poking fun at the learned sober-minded reader by imitating his pretentious, complicated sentence structure and signing the document as "Jeremias Müller, Lic. Dr." Thus he added to a very common family name a given name reminiscent of the Old Testament figure that is famous for his ominous prophecies. He also conferred on him the higest German academic degree in the field of religion.

The cover of the first edition of the *Galgenlieder* shows the hill with the gallows and the fellows dangling from them. A flock of ravens is seen in the background. The first part of the book deals with the fraternity of the gallows. Their anthem originally opened the collection:

> Bundeslied der Galgenbrüder
> O schauerliche Lebenswirrn,
> wir hängen hier am roten Zwirn!
> Die Unke unkt, die Spinne spinnt,
> und schiefe Scheitel kämmt der Wind.

The last lines read:

> Es schreit der Kauz: pardauz, pardauz!
> Da tauts, da grauts, da brauts, da blauts!

> Chorus of the Gallows Gang
> O life of horror-stricken dread!
> We dangle from the crimson thread.
> The spider spins, the croaker croaks
> and skewy skulls the night wind strokes.
> . . . .
> The hooter hoots his weird hoo-hoos.
> It dawns and dews and brews and blues.[2]

What Morgenstern actually describes here are the horrified shivers of the hanged victims, intensified by the uncanny sounds of some loathsome animals heard through the night until the break of day. Yet, as we listen to these lines, we feel the playful evocation of a gruesome mood, for the fellows are hanged not with a sturdy rope but with a red thread, and the nightwind plays with the curls on their drooping heads. The very next song is, at the same time, much more gruesome in its realistic details and more playful in the imagi-

nary love call of the skeleton hanging from the gallows addressed to
the hangman's admired lass:

Galgenbruders Lied an Sophie, die Henkersmaid

> Sophie, mein Henkersmädel,
> komm, küsse mir den Schädel!
> Zwar ist mein Mund
> ein schwarzer Schlund—
> doch du bist gut und edel!
>
> Sophie, mein Henkersmädel,
> komm, streichle mir den Schädel!
> Zwar ist mein Haupt
> des Haars beraubt—
> doch du bist gut und edel!
>
> Sophie, mein Henkersmädel,
> komm, schau mir in den Schädel!
> Die Augen zwar,
> sie frass der Aar—
> doch du bist gut und edel!

The Hanged Man's Song to the Hangman's Maid

> Sophia, hangman's mate,
> O come and kiss my pate!
> My mouth now is
> a black abyss—
> but you are nobly great!
>
> Sophia, hangman's mate,
> O come, caress my pate!
> My skull is bare
> and lacking hair—
> but you are nobly great!
>
> Sophia, hangman's mate,
> O come, behold my pate!
> The eagle flies—

he picked my eyes.
But you are nobly great.[3]

At the threshold of the intellectual age that was dominated by
physics and chemistry, Morgenstern gave his *Galgenlieder* the fol-
lowing motto: "Let the molecules race, no matter what they come
up with, quit the quibbling and refining, keep the ecstasies invio-
late." And then he named the hangman's helper Sophia, the Greek
word for wisdom. Was that a profundity, or did the poet simply want
to pull the philosophically minded interpreter's leg? Just as gro-
tesque as the conversation of the skeleton are the sentiments ex-
pressed in "Galgenbruders Frühlingslied" ("Gallows Fellow's
Spring Song"), for the dangling fellow who rejoices over the coming
of spring as he discovers a little blade sprouting in the knothole of
the gallows beam is already dead. His condition is revealed as a
surprise at the end. Not so in the other song entitled "Des Galgen-
bruders Gebet und Erhörung" ("The Gallows Fellow's Prayer and
Its Fulfillment"), because here Morgenstern adds the stage direc-
tion: to be sung in the other world. And yet this doomed man still
seems to be very much part of the physical world because he is
annoyed by an incessant croaking, the thinking aloud of a frog. He
appeals to the Almighty to silence the animal which, in turn, tells
the fellow to shut his mouth or else the silver horse will eat him up
like oats. The outcome is uncertain. The poet simply states that
fifteen minutes later the silver horse appeared in the reed patch. At
any rate, we must conclude that the departed soul is haunting the
scene of the hanging. This episode is not among the original
Galgenlieder, but the nocturnal scenery is the same as in the "Bun-
deslied" ("fraternal anthem") quoted above where the silver horses
are mentioned. The time is near midnight when not only departed
souls but other weird creatures as well make their appearance,
among them the elf which is a product of Morgenstern's linguistic
inventiveness. It is the elf that announces the spirit hour at twelve.
He is, therefore, called the Zwölf-Elf. He is introduced this way:
"Der Zwölf-Elf hebt die linke Hand:/ Da schlägt es Mitternacht im
Land" ("The twelve nix raises his left hand, then midnight strikes
throughout the land"). We hear how the animals perk up: the bit-

tern, the snail, the potato mouse, the will-o'-the-wisp, while the canyon dog barks softly. The two moles kiss each other on the snout. A malicious sprite shakes his fist because a late hiker did not get lost in the bog. Sophia, the hangman's girl, has a nightmare, the gallows gang sways to and fro, and the raven Ralph cries ominously: the end has come: "Der Zwölf-Elf senkt die linke Hand: / Und wieder schläft das ganze land" ("The twelve nix lowers his left hand, and again asleep is all the land"). How the raven Ralph caused his own end by furtively nibbling at gallows food which is poisonous is told in a song "Der Rabe Ralph" as a hush-hush tale with many still stills and hoo hoos. In a later poem entitled "Das Problem" we learn that the Zwölf-Elf no longer likes his name. What it really amounts to is twenty-three. So he adopts this name from now on.

In addition to the midnight mouse and the potato mouse, Morgenstern's linguistic imagination created other unheard of creatures: the Zwölf-Elf's child called Sechs-Elf, the Nachtalp (nightingale) Henne (the nocturnal Alpine Hen), the Uhuin (the She-owl), the Nachtwindhund, the Siebenschwein (the Sevenswine), and the Nachtschelm (the Night Rogue). The latter two were married happily. The others are mentioned more casually, the moonsheep's fate, however, is described in greater detail. The moonsheep gets tired waiting to be shorn up there on the moon and walks to its Alpine pasture. It dreams of the dark vastness of the universe. In the morning, the moon is gone, and that is the end of the moonsheep. The style adopted by the poet is that of the popular ballad: "Das Mondschaf liegt am Morgen tot./ Sein Leib ist weiss, die Sonn' ist rot" ("In the morning the moonsheep lies dead. Its body is white, the sun is red"). As if to counteract this folksy style, Morgenstern added a translation in Latin rhymes that are somewhat less than classic. The Latin poem is called "Lunovis."

The creation of a new fabulous animal through linguistic manipulation is well illustrated in "Das Geierlamm," included in *Alle Galgenlieder*. While most of the other new animals are created by combining two disparate components, such as moon and sheep, the linguistic trick here is the reversal of the sequence of two already existing composite parts. In this manner we get, instead of the forthright bird of prey called Lämmergeier, something like a wolf in sheep's clothing. The style of the poem is alarmingly, or rather disarmingly, simple in view of its forbidding contents:

Das Geierlamm

Der Lämmergeier ist bekannt,
das Geierlamm erst hier genannt.

Der Geier, der ist offenkundig,
das Lamm hingegen untergrundig.

Es sagt nicht hu, es sagt nicht mäh
und frisst dich auf aus nächster Näh.

Und dreht das Auge dann zum Herrn.
Und alle habens herzlich gern.

The Hawken Chick

The Chicken hawk is widely known;
the Hawken chick is all my own.

The Hawk swoops down rapaciously;
the Chick does things more graciously.

It does not cluck, it does not coo;
but when you're close, it swallows you,

then stands so innocent and mute
that all are saying: "My, how cute!"[4]

In his poem "Das Nasobēm" an entirely fictitious animal is created by Morgenstern right before our eyes. As it stalks past us accompanied by its offspring, walking on its several noses, we are reminded of some prehistoric odd-shaped monster, but it actually "stepped forth from the poet's lyre into the light of day." Another imaginary wild animal is described in the poem "Der Steinochs" ("stone Ox"), probably conceived in contrast to the much more timid *Steinbock* ("ibex"). Both have long horns and roam the world

of the high Alps. While the *Steinbock* shies away from the confronta-
tion with humans, the *Steinochs* attacks them, ramming its long
horn right through them. It feeds on the hay of human brains. Being
of stone, it is indestructible, while we mortals will crumble to dust.
The unicorn is a legendary animal which lives among us, here and
there, as the name of an inn. Perhaps some day we human beings
will become legendary also and lend our name to a hotel at the sign
of "the golden man." Such is Morgenstern's reasoning in his poem
"Das Einhorn."

The fantastic element that characterizes many of the foregoing
poems about animals is absent in some others in which the animals
reveal base human traits, as in the story of the porcupine from Siam,
which is so enraged at the sight of a man that it shoots all its spines at
him, thus fastening him to a tree like Saint Sebastian. Then, de-
prived of its spines, a horrible sight, it slinks back into the jungle to
repent. The two donkeys in the poem "Die beiden Esel" ("The Two
Donkeys") are all too human:

> Ein finstrer Esel sprach einmal
> zu seinem ehlichen Gemahl:
>
> "Ich bin so dumm, du bist so dumm,
> wir wollen sterben gehen, kumm!"
>
> Doch wie es kommt so öfter eben:
> Die beiden blieben fröhlich leben.
>
> A gloomy donkey, tir'd of life
> one day addressed his wedded wife:
>
> "I am so dumb, you are so dumb,
> let's go and die together, come!"
>
> But as befalls, time and again,
> they lived on happily, the twain.[5]

Jealousy, a human quality, is certainly also found in animals, but
the description of the psychosomatic effects as presented by
Morgenstern in the poem "Der heroische Pudel" is in the vein of his
humor. A black poodle feeling neglected during the protracted

piano playing of his mistress in spite of his howling becomes so grief-stricken that when he gets up at the crack of dawn next morning his hair has turned a silvery white. In the poem "Der Droschkengaul" the casual observation of a lowly hack horse induces the poet to attribute to this animal a distinctly human outlook. When he takes a rest from his pulling the feed bag is tied around his neck. As he swings it back and forth, probing its contents, he does not succeed in getting to the bottom of it all. There are always some crumbs left. Meditating as he munches, he comes to the conclusion that earthly skill and knowledge are limited.

In German script, the capital letters *N* and *ST* look almost identical. Therefore, the *Nilpferd* ("Nile horse") in the poem bearing its name feels crushed when it sees its name spelled *Stilpferd* ("style horse") and when it is promptly adopted by the esthetes as part of their coat of arms. Although it was not taught the German script, it pines away over this error. It becomes extinct and its name is replaced by the foreign word hippopotamus. Apprehension over its extinction may have caused the lion in the poem "Der Leu" ("The Lion") to permit its picture to appear on the calendar:

Auf einem Wandkalenderblatt
ein Leu sich abgebildet hat.

Er blickt dich an bewegt und still
den ganzen 17. April.

Wodurch er zu erinnern liebt,
dass es ihn immerhin noch gibt.

A leaf of a calendar on the wall
displays a lion, grand and tall.

He views you regal and serene
the whole of April seventeen.

Reminding you, lest you forget,
that he is not extinct as yet.[6]

It is an old literary tradition that the animal fable should teach a lesson to readers by providing an illustration from the animal kingdom. For the *Galgenlieder* we have Morgenstern's exhortation to approach them naively and leave sophistication behind. Nevertheless, in many of them social criticism is implied no matter how charmingly disguised. In fact, the clever disguise is what the reader enjoys. Of course, there are different degrees of transparency. In a poem like "Der Hahn" ("The Cock"), social criticism contains a pinch of sarcasm which is very rare in the *Galgenlieder*. We hear of a cock that outrages society by his deviation from the natural order of things: he has laid an egg. This happened in Basel. Such localization is unusual in Morgenstern's poetry. Perhaps this city is mentioned not because it is the original home of Paracelsus, who proclaimed the wisdom of nature and advised the physician to strengthen nature's purposes; rather, it probably stands for a city with a strong and old cultural tradition. The cock is duly incarcerated and, unrepentant, stands trial, is tortured, and, finally condemned to be burned at the stake. There the assembled crowd sings a hymn of praise for the salvation of the cock. Someone suddenly cries out: down on your knees in gratitude to God. This spectator believes that he has heard the cock change his tune from the pitiful kikiriki (cock-a-doodle-doo) to Kyrie eleison.

While society's intolerance is ridiculed in the poem about the cock, society's wastefulness in its affluence, for the unintentional benefit of the cock pigeon, is pictured with good-natured charm in the poem "Der Grossstadttauber" ("The metropolitan station cock pigeon"). This half-domesticated bird picks up the leavings from wherever the good Lord sends them to him: one tenth of a cornet from Salzburg, the scrap of a frank from Frankfurt, an applecore from Bolzano, and a bit of cheese from the Abruzzi. Thus it participates in the living standards of Germany and other countries, whatever these may be. Talking about a station and a feathered creature, we are immediately reminded of that well-known *Galgenlied* entitled "Das Huhn" ("The Hen"):

> In der Bahnhofhalle, nicht für es gebaut,
> geht ein Huhn

hin und her. . . .
Wo, wo ist der Herr Stationsversteh'r?
Wird dem Huhn
man nichts tun?
Hoffen wir es! Sagen wir es laut:
dass ihm unsre Sympathie gehört,
selbst an dieser Stätte, wo es—"stört"!

In the railroad station, never built for her,
walks a hen
to and fro.
Where, where did the station master go?
Will not men
harm the hen?
Let's hope *not*. Let's candidly aver
that our sympathy she still enjoys,
even in this place, where she annoys.[7]

If we keep in mind that the railway stations in the German Empire
were government property, that there was a craze for orderliness in
public places enforced by posted regulations, and that the chain of
command and the respective responsibility was strictly observed,
we can appreciate the delicacy of the situation described and the
reason why this particular poem became so popular.

At the end of this presentation of the animal world in the *Galgen-
lieder* we may place "Fisches Nachtgesang" ("Lullaby of the Fish").
These creatures, mute as they are, make a silent contribution to the
collection when they open and close their jaws in accordance with
the rhythmic pattern devised by the poet:

$$—$$
$$— \; — \; —$$
$$— \; — \; —$$
$$— \; — \; —$$
$$— \; — \; —$$
$$— \; — \; —$$
$$—$$

In the German Empire, the authority of even minor government officials was respectfully accepted by the general public, provided it was exercised within their sphere of competence. Gerhart Hauptmann, in some of his comedies such as *Der Biberpelz*, successfully pilloried the arrogance of government officials who took advantage of the docile attitude of law-abiding citizens. In some rural areas, the public schoolteacher was, next to the clergyman, the only educated person in the village and wielded considerable power over the minds of obedient citizens. At any rate, in such erudite a subject such as the grammar of the native tongue he was an undisputed authority. Therefore, a creature of low social standing who got the absurd notion that his name could be made the subject of grammatical inflection would naturally turn to the schoolteacher. If this creature was the legendary werewolf, that is, a human being transformed into a wolf by witchcraft, he could, as an outlaw of society, make his appearance only at night. In the spirit hour he could communicate with the departed spirit of the schoolteacher. Squatting at the grave site, with his paws crossed, he pleads to have his name inflected. The schoolteacher, emphasizing his superior status by climbing on the knob crowning the metal plate erected over his grave, pompously recites the four cases in the singular: *der Werwolf, des Weswolfs*, etc. The werewolf feels flattered by the various cases and asks for the plural forms. But the schoolteacher regretfully informs him that *wer* ("who") occurs only in the singular. The werewolf gets up, his eyes blinded by tears, for he has a wife and children. But since he is not a learned person he takes his leave with humble thanks.

The ancient, traditional justification for the existence of literature, that it should instruct while it delights, does not apply to the *Galgenlieder*. According to Morgenstern's own opinion, the poems should delight through their charm and playfulness. Any effort at improving man or society is merely coincidental. We found social criticism charmingly disguised in "Der Hahn." Morgenstern mitigated the implied censure by calling the fable a *Teufelslegendchen* ("a devil's little tale"). Both a schoolteacher and a stationmaster are representatives of the state, but the role which the former plays in "Werwolf" is that of an obliging ghost, and in "Das Huhn" the latter is an authority not even available when he is needed. As if to make up for this apparent gap in the picture of the German railway system, Morgenstern presents a small-town stationmaster glorying in the fullness of his responsibility as he directs an express train, a suburban train, and a freight train almost simultaneously, feeling like a little Napoleon in "Der Bahnhofvorstand" ("The Stationmaster"). The thoroughgoing inquisitiveness of the German police which, as an organ of the government, was already ridiculed by Lessing in his comedy *Minna von Barnhelm* (1767) is reflected in the contents and style of the questionnaire which is sent to Mr. Korf and answered by him in like manner in one of the funniest poems in this collection: "Die Behörde" ("The Authorities").

When human beings are portrayed in the *Galgenlieder*, they are usually "little people." Morgenstern describes the trials and tribulations of the housemaid with a sympathetic heart, now from the standpoint of the servant girl and then again from the point of view of the employer, In "Mägde am Sonnabend" ("Servant Girls on Saturday") we witness with what relish and fury the girls beat the carpets and runners to vent their pent-up resentment at the humiliation they had to endure during the past week. Two poems called "Zäzile" ("Cecily") are devoted to this unlucky housemaid. An inborn sense of orderliness drives Cecily to action when she enters the study of her master and sees books lying around on tables, and chairs and papers of all kinds scattered about in apparent disarray. She restacks books and papers according to size and shape. The despair of her master is not put into words. Not so in the other poem, where her mistress announces bluntly that this maid must go. What has happened? Cecily was supposed to clean the windows so thoroughly that, in the words of her mistress, you could not tell whether you were looking through glass or through air. After several attempts to attain this ideal condition she became so enraged that she smashed the glass and removed all traces of it from the frames. Her mistress, first taken aback by her maid's success, did not take long to discover the awful truth.

Both the simplicity of heart and the requirement of obedience link Cecily to the nuns whom Morgenstern portrays in the poem "St. Expeditus." Again and again crates with fresh fruit, cakes, garden tools, and wearing apparel would arrive at a nunnery in Rome. On each crate the word ESPEDITO was printed in large letters. At first the nuns were puzzled, since they did not know the generous donor. Finally one sister had an idea: the donor must be a saint named Expeditus. Now an artist was commissioned to paint the saint with the crate. Tablets and candles were dedicated to him, and he was worshipped by many who received gifts. Then, in 1905, the Vatican investigated and decreed that there was no such saint. But the German poet could not accept this official verdict. He still imagined him with his white hair, kind eyes, and jolly gestures, some kind of Santa Claus when surrounded by his faithful nuns, showers gifts on poor children while the Blessed Virgin looks down from heaven and gives her blessing.

High boots, worn nowadays primarily by horsemen, used to be a common footgear for travel and work in the fields. A wooden forked instrument employed to hold the boot by the heel while the wearer withdraws his foot is called *Stiefelknecht* ("bootjack"). In "Gingganz" Morgenstern shows us a boot, accompanied by his bootjack, walking from one village to the next. Lost in thought, the boot suddenly stops and asks the bootjack to pull him off. Off whom? the other inquires, puzzled. The boot, aroused from his daydreaming, admits that he has been befuddled ever since he lost his master. Thereupon the bootjack throws up his arms in frustration, and the two start trudging on again. The strange title of this poem is derived from two successive words taken from the first line of the fifth stanza: "Ich ging ganz in Gedanken hin" ("I walked along all lost in thought").

The high-spirited glorification of a lowly wearing apparel on the clothes line is found in

"Die Unterhose"

Heilig ist die Unterhose,
wenn sie sich in Sonn und Wind,
frei von ihrem Alltagslose,
auf ihr wahres Selbst besinnt.

Fröhlich ledig der Blamage
steter Souterränität,
wirkt am Seil sie als Staffage,
wie ein Segel leicht gebläht.

Holy is the underwear when it becomes aware of its true self in sun and
wind, free from its daily drudgery. Happily released from the disgrace of
always being an underling, it hangs like a stage decoration, gracefully bil-
lowing like a sail.

The ghostly animation of the whole array of garments is described
in "Ein modernes Märchen" ("A Modern Fairytale"). Wardrobes
open of their own accord in the dark house. Frock coats, trousers,
and dresses are strutting about, sitting, and resting on armchairs
and couches; but they are without heads and hands, gesturing in
silence to each other. When the clock strikes one, they hurry back
to their wardrobes except for one lacy blouse that is caught at a
window hook and desperately tries to get disentangled because it
feels exposed to the bright moonlight. Lured by its soft whimper, a
sleepwalker comes floating in from the adjoining bedroom. With a
steady hand she frees the trembling blouse and puts it back on its
hanger. The following poem likewise presents a nocturnal scene,
but the animation is not confined to the spirit hour. Nothing exciting
happens, except that a walk through the forest is taken by two
funnels. The special feature here is that the arrangement of lines
actually reproduces the shape of a funnel:

Zwei Trichter wandeln durch die Nacht.
Durch ihres Rumpfs verengten Schacht
fliesst weisses Mondlicht
still und heiter
auf ihren
Waldweg
u. s.
w.

Two funnels travel through the night;
a sylvan moon's candescent light
employs their bodies' narrow

flue in flowing pale
and cheerful
thro
ug
h[8]

Animation progresses as Morgenstern moves from the visual to
the auditory sphere, from picture to sound. A well-known example
of the latter is the poem "Bim, Bam, Bum" ("Ding, Dang, Dong").
This is the story of the ringing of the bells, each of which has its own
pitch. A bell sound dang flies through the night in search of his lady
bell sound ding who has been unfaithful to him. "Please, come
back," he cries out, "your dong awaits you anxiously." But ding was
eloping with dang and could not be found by dong because he was
flying in the wrong direction. Still more ethereal than the sound of a
church bell is a sigh that comes from a young heart in love. And
Morgenstern's description of its activity, in the poem called "Der
Seufzer" ("The Sigh"), is even more grotesque. It happens on a
moonlit night when the sigh is skating outside the city wall. Ardent
desire seizes him as he thinks of his young sweetheart. He stops
and—the ice melts under his skates. He sinks and is never seen
again.

Moving away from the domain of things seen or heard, we now
reach a uniquely Morgensternian sphere that can only be ap-
proached by way of linguistic trickery. The trick is to isolate some-
thing that can exist only as an integral part of a higher entity or that
exists only in relationship to something else. The following four
poems may serve as examples: "Das Knie" ("The Knee"), "Der Saal"
("The Hall"), "Der Lattenzaun" ("The Picket Fence"), and "Die
Westküsten" ("The Westcoasts"). In the first poem, Morgenstern
assures us that he is only talking about a knee. The rest of the
soldier's body has been destroyed by cannon or rifle fire. The sec-
ond poem tells about a jewel thief who does not mind stealing other
things, such as shoes or shirts. But one day he steals—it is hard to
believe—an entire hall that happens to be unused. It is located on
the second floor of a house in a busy downtown section. The thief
gains entry through a room above simply by breaking through the

ceiling. For the time being he hides the stolen hall on a boat in the Spree River. The guard on the river bank watches with a friendly smile as the thief approaches with his cart. One day in July he starts out in the direction of Hamburg, only to sail from there across the Atlantic to Baltimore. The thief travels to the West with the stolen hall on display. Meanwhile, at home, even the oldest policeman does not know what to do. The place of the crime looks very desolate. The bizarre situation arises because a hall with its walls, its floor, and its ceiling can only exist as part of a building. The same applies to a picket fence which has its pickets fastened to a horizontal bar at regular intervals. When the builder removes the intervals and builds a large house with them, the fence looks so impossible that the state confiscates it. The builder, however, has to flee overseas.

The west coasts are tired of being named after their geographical location. They want to be independent from arbitrary domination by man. So they call a conference to consider the means for their liberation. Some Asiatic coasts point out that even if they could do away with man there would still be the maps. Finally they summon five hundred *Tintenfische* ("inkfish," "cuttlefish") and draw up a resolution to the effect that there is no such thing as a west coast. They make this resolution known everywhere; to the seagulls, who laughed, to the clouds, who were too far away, to the whale, who ignored it. "Aren't you a whale, you fool?" they ask. "Quite correct," he replies calmly, "but your thinking makes me into one." The coasts start to reflect, and their reflection gives them an uncanny feeling. They quietly float home, each to his own country, and the resolution is never sent out. Through linguistic manipulation Morgenstern succeeds in creating something that actually does not exist. We must assume that the united coasts of this globe have left their location and have a meeting in mid-ocean, because at the end of the conference they quietly float home. Nevertheless, they insist that they do not exist because, in their desire for freedom, they do not want to be tagged, and they feel that they exist only by virtue of the name bestowed on them by man. This is true. The name *Küste* merely indicates the transition from sea to land. It is impossible to think of the coast as something separated from the land. If they should break loose, they would sink to the bottom of the ocean and become part of the sea floor, or else they would float away as islands. In short, the coastline is merely a human designation.

In the poem "Die Nähe" ("Proximity") a strange grammatical device is used by Morgenstern to transform an abstract noun into a living being. Grief-stricken proximity walks around as if in a trance because she can never come to grips with the real things. She grows thinner and thinner, and her face turns evermore yellow. One night she hears a voice in her sleep: "Rise, my child. I am the categorical comparative. I shall raise you to the comparative form *Näher* ["nearer"] or, if you wish, to its feminine *Näherin* ["seamstress," derived from the verb *nähen,* to sew"]. Proximity does not refuse, but accepts the offer as her fate. But as a seamstress she unfortunately forgets what she used to be. She calls herself Mrs. Nolte, does millinery work, and even considers her former existence to be a joke.

In creating new creatures linguistically, Morgenstern's mental association was often guided by the sound of the word rather than its meaning, as in *Nähe—Näher—Näherin.* Sometimes he must have felt that the language was leading him on and that he was merely its agent. This idea is presented in the poem "Der Purzelbaum" ("The Somersault"). Most Germans hearing this word understand the first part because it comes from the verb *purzeln* ("to tumble"). But *Baum* ("tree") does not make any sense in this combination. Etymologically, it is connected with *sich bäumen* ("to rear," as a horse may do). If you do so with too much force, you turn a somersault. If you do it unintentionally, that is, if you are thrown, you may feel that some higher power is using you. This is the underlying thought of this poem, which shows us a somersault with an inferiority complex coming to the poet and displaying a lack of self-respect. As a tree, he does not bear fruit and has no roots. Moreover, he does not perform but is being performed. "As soon as I tumble, all that is left is a *Purzeltraum* ["a tumble's dream"]. "Just look at us," says the poet, "we are no better off, we have no roots, we bear no fruit": "wir schiessen nicht, es schiesst uns" ("we don't do the performing, the performance is done through us"). "Go home to your tumblewoods and don't slander your own kind." Germans who like to quote

Morgenstern often use this phrase: "Wir schiessen nicht, es schiesst uns," meaning that they have lost control over a situation.

If playing with the language is the primary driving force in the *Galgenlieder* and if language strikes the ear as a sequence of vowels and consonants, the ultimate goal would be for the *Galgenlieder* to have no other aim than to stimulate and please our ear. For the fraternity of the gallows, Morgenstern created such a humorous song and called it "Das grosse Lalulā" ("The Great Lalula"):

> Kroklokwafzi? Sememēmi!
> Seiokrontro—prafriplo:
> Bifzi, bafzi; hulalēmi:
> quasti basti bo. . . .
> Lalu, lalu lalu lalu la!
>
> Nontraruru miromente
> zasku zes rü rü?
> Entepente, leiolente
> klekwapufzi lü?
> Lalu lalu lalu lalu la!
>
> Simarar kos malzipempu
> silzuzankunkrei (;)!
> Marjomar dos: Quempu Lempu
> Siri Suri Sei[]!
> Lalu lalu lalu lalu la!

We remember that, in his eagerness for new sound effects, Morgenstern as a boy invented a secret language for his intimate friends and that later he studied Volapük, a contrived universal language which enjoyed popularity in the 1880s.

The *Galgenlieder*, of which we could describe only a selected few are the product of a highly imaginative mind that gives full sway to its fancies which, however, have a coherence and organic development of their own. Here we get a different world. Morgenstern says: "From the gallows hill you see the world differently and you see different things than others do." An adult uses language as a tool for communicating with others and describing the world as it is. In the gallows songs, language appears as a creative force. It links the empirical world with a world of fancy. Things of our daily life become animated: a boot, a funnel, a hall. As in fairy tales, animals have human feelings and can talk: a hack horse, a donkey, a porcupine, a hippopotamus. New creatures are created linguistically: a twelve nix, a moonsheep, a hawken chick, a nasobem. The Gingganz, Morgenstern explains to a puzzled critic, is a dreamer or ideologist. Abstract concepts take on bodily form: proximity philosophizes about its mission and is changed into a seamstress. A somersault is dissatisfied with himself, and a sigh goes skating. This language creates matter out of thin air: the open spaces between the pickets of a picket fence are used as building material. Thus Morgenstern describes not only a potential world, as we shall see in *Palmström*, but he also bestows existence upon the impossible. This is the magic attraction of the *Galgenlieder* and the secret source of their popularity. Morgenstern wanted to loosen up the dull, dismal seriousness to which man was tied in a materialistic contemporary world. He wanted to stimulate the imagination and spread a spirit of levity, cheerfulness, and freedom; and in this he was singularly successful. Although the authoritative literary critics of the day, with few exceptions, did not know what to do do with the *Galgenlieder* and did not mind saying so, the general public took to them and gave them an enthusiastic reception. Morgenstern felt encouraged to continue in the same vein and hoped to publish a second volume within two or three years.

But his publisher Bruno Cassirer was afraid that this would be too much of a good thing. Nevertheless, the poet kept at it, off and on, for his own enjoyment. Finally, after four years, having published some beautiful lyrics of a serious nature in the meantime, Morgenstern presented another collection of grotesque poems to the delighted Cassirer, and so *Palmström* came out in the spring of 1910. Tenderhearted Palmström and his like-minded friend von Korf are not only imaginary but very imaginative characters. Unconcerned about the realities of life, they live in a world of their own. They share one feature with Till Eulenspiegel, the prankster in the old German folk tales: they often take metaphors literally. The best-known example is the poem "Die weggeworfene Flinte" ("The Abandoned Rifle"). It is based on the phrase "die Flinte ins

Korn werfen" ("to throw one's rifle into the wheat field"), indicating that a person abandons his undertaking. Roaming along a wheat field one evening, Palmström catches sight of a rifle that had been thrown away between the stalks. He stops his carefree singing and sadly sits down to examine his find. Picturing the despondent man who threw his rifle away, Palmström commiserates with him. He decorates the barrel and the butt with poppy and the spikes of the wheat and leans it against the nearest road sign, hoping that the fainthearted man would pass by again. A charming example of human sympathy and understanding for an unknown fellow man.

Linguistic imagination creates an odd garment in the poem "Die Oste." It is invented as a counterpart to *die Weste,* a waistcoat to be worn under the jacket and visible in front, sometimes made of fancy material with pockets for a watch and other valuables. Why should our stomach be privileged to be covered with flower patterns and fancy buttons and pockets? Let's have equality, Palmström argues, and wear such a garment on our back, an eastcoat. Lo and behold! The tailors take up the idea in no time and produce a hundred thousand such pieces of clothing before they go out of fashion. Korf dreams of another invention: "Die Tagnachtlampe" ("The Daynight Lamp"). A humorous effect is achieved by Morgenstern's parenthetical style:

> Korf erfindet eine Tagnachtlampe,
> die, sobald sie angedreht,
> selbst den hellsten Tag
> in Nacht verwandelt.
>
> Als er sie vor des Kongresses Rampe
> demonstriert, vermag
> niemand, der sein Fach versteht,
> zu verkennen, dass es sich hier handelt—
>
> (Finster wirds am hellerlichten Tag,
> und ein Beifallssturm das Haus durchweht.)
> (Und man ruft dem Diener Mampe:
> "Licht anzünden!")—dass es sich hier handelt

um das Faktum: dass gedachte Lampe,
in der Tat, wenn angedreht,
selbst den hellsten Tag
in Nacht verwandelt.

The Daynight Lamp
Korf invents a daynight lamp
which, as soon as operated,
turns the brightest day
into night.

When he demonstrates it on the ramp
of Convention Hall, no expert may
gainsay, if he's not opinionated,
that one finds it quite. . . .

(Darkness falls upon the sunlit day;
delegates are clapping, fascinated,
and one calls to Butler Bramp:
"Turn the light on!")—that one finds it quite

evident that the invented lamp
will indeed when operated
turn the brightest day
into night.[9]

Another fantastic invention by Palmström is described in the poem "Die Geruchs-Orgel." Palmström builds an olfactory organ and plays on it von Korf's *Nieswurz-Sonate* ("sneezewort," that is, hellebore, sonata). It opens with Alpine herbs followed by an aria of acacias. The notorious sneezewort phrases give the sonata its name. The "Ha-Cis-Synkopen" (B–C major syncopations) make Palmström nearly fall from his chair while von Korf sits safely at home, dashing off one opus after another. Inspired by von Korf's sonata, friends later find an automat for all kinds of aromas. You insert a coin, and a balmy trumpet blows the desired aroma into your distended nostrils, while a pertinent image appears on the screen. Hundreds of guests are now enjoying their meals more than ever, we are told in this poem, "Der Aromat" ("The Aromat"). For studious people von Korf invents a daily newspaper that comes out at noon. When you read all of it you have had enough, and no other food is necessary. All smart people are subscribing to this newspaper, as we are told in the poem "Die Mittagszeitung" ("The Noonday Paper"). Korf is annoyed by the verbosity of many contemporary authors. Reading them consumes too much time. In order to increase his reading speed he invents glasses that contract the text. A poem like this one called "Die Brille" ("The Eyeglasses") would be disregarded in such a contracted text, and thirty-three of them would amount merely to a question mark.

There are a number of poems telling about episodes from the lives of the two friends. The following three have become famous: "Die Mausefalle" ("The Mousetrap"), "Das Warenhaus" ("The Department Store"), "Die unmögliche Tatsache" ("The Impossible Fact"). Palmström has a mouse in his house but no mousetrap. Korf constructs a trap from wires. Then he places Palmström inside, with a violin to lure the rodent. Palmström plays in the dark, and the mouse walks in. The sensitive trapdoor shuts behind it. Palmström soon falls asleep. The next morning the whole contraption is loaded on a horse-drawn truck and carted to a distant clearing. There the two captives are released. The animal rejoices over the new surroundings while Palmström rides home with his friend, serenely happy.

Palmström cannot live without mail. Every day he tensely waits for the mailman, but rarely does he hear a letter drop into the mailbox. Finally he remembers that he could order, for three months, miscellaneous mail from the department store. Now he is getting all kinds of assorted mail. Everyone seems to think of him. He feels that he is placed at the hub of the world, and this thought makes him dizzy until he remembers that it is merely what he ordered from the department store. This poem is made up of terza rimas. The first and the third lines of each stanza rhyme while the second, consisting of one word only, does not.

The aging Palmström has been run over by a motor vehicle. Determined to go on living, he gets up and wonders how this accident could have happened at all. Who is to blame—the state for not issuing proper laws, the police for allowing the cars to come through here? Wrapped in wet sheets, he consults books of law and concludes that no cars were allowed at that spot. It seems to him now that he experienced the whole incident in his dream. It is "an impossible fact," " 'Weil,' so schliesst er messerscharf,/ nicht sein *kann*, was nicht sein *darf* (" 'Because,' as he concludes with great precision, 'that which *must not* be, *can not* be' ").

A few poems in the collection are connected with Palmström's aunt Palma Kunkel (distaff). She wants to remain anonymous and keeps young by not wasting her breath on inane conversation. She would not appreciate those of the gallows songs that do not convey any intelligible meaning but revel in sound, such as the poem "Notturno in Weiss" ("Nocturne in White").

> Die steinerne Familie,
> aus Marmelstein gemacht,
> sie kniet um eine Lilie,
> im Kreis um eine Lilie
> in totenstiller Nacht.
>
> Der Lilie Weiss ist weicher
> als wie das Weiss des Steins,
> der Lilie Weiss ist weicher,
> doch das des Steins ist bleicher
> im Weiss des Mondenscheins.
>
> Die Lilie, die Familie,
> der Mond in sanfter Pracht,
> sie halten so Vigilie,
> wetteifernde Vigilie
> in totenstiller Nacht.

A family of stone, made of marble, kneels around a lily, in a circle around a lily in a deathly silent night. The white of the lily is softer than the white of the stone, the white of the lily is softer, but that of the stone is paler in the white of the moonlight. The lily, the family, the moon in its soft splendor thus keep their vigil outdoing each other in the deathly silence of the night.

This moonlit graveyard scene reminds us of the fact that the poem was written in the heyday of neo-romanticism with its penchant for sonorous verse.

Concerning the verse form of the *Galgenlieder,* we notice that the quatrains are the most common, while terza rima is less frequently used. As a matter of fact, a great variety of stanzas can be found, some having five, six, seven, eight, nine, twelve, fourteen, sixteen, and even eighteen lines. Those of eight lines or more could have been broken up into two or more stanzas, because in Morgenstern's poetry one line often runs over into the next (enjambment), which occasionally applies to stanzas as well. Having unimportant words such as "and" or "which" provide the rhyme is a characteristic of his poetic style. A few times he even goes so far as to place the first half of a word at the end of the line with the last half opening the next line. The best-known example occurs in his poem "Das aesthetische Wiesel" ("The Aesthetic Weasel"):

Ein Wiesel
sass auf einem Kiesel
inmitten Bachgeriesel.

Wisst ihr,
Weshalb?

Das Mondkalb
verriet es mir
im Stillen:

Das raffinier-
te Tier
tats um des Reimes willen.

A weasel
perched on an easel
within a patch of teasel.

But why
and how?

The moon cow
whispered her reply
one time:

> The sopheest-
> icated beest
> did it just for the rhyme.[10]

The number of Palmström poems with stanzas of varying length is small. Very few poems are unrhymed. On the other hand, many others that have rhymes read like prose because of the matter-of-factness of their diction, which puts their humor into relief.

At the end of *Alle Galgenlieder*, we find a few selected passages in prose, supposedly clippings from the press. The following is a choice selection:

Artificial heads! Everyone who does not buy an artificial head is a fool. The artificial head is superimposed on the natural one and affords, in comparison with the latter, the following advantages: (a) protection against the rain, wind, sun, dust, in short, all external abuses that inconvenience the natural head unceasingly and keep it from its real occupation of thinking, (b) enhancement of the functions of the natural senses. With your artificial ears you hear a hundred times better than with the natural ones. One sees with the vision device as clearly as with a binocular. With the a. h. [The German text uses K. K. for *künstlicher Kopf*. This was in Prussia an abbreviation for the designation of a government office, that is, *kaiserlich königlich* since the king of Prussia was also the German emperor. Through this abbreviation the product, by mental association, seems to receive government sanction.] you can smell more keenly and have a more discriminating taste than with its predecessor. But you don't need any of this. You can regulate the apparatus as you wish, including zero function. The a. h. that is put on zero makes a completely undisturbed inner life possible. Locked rooms, monk's cells, the solitude of the woods, etc. are henceforth superfluous. You can isolate yourself in the densest crowd. The a. h. is available only custommade and is easy to wear. It is protected by a special battery against unauthorized touching. Since it needs no hair covering, the skull can be used as advertising space. If you are smart and unprejudiced, you can easily recover the expense of an a. h. by accepting an advertisement from an appropriately large firm. You can even earn money more easily in this manner than with your natural head.

On the last page of *Alle Galgenlieder* we find the following

Announcement
Nov. 22 Fritz Mauthner Day Nov. 22
Grand Spectacle
Big Word Kill Prizes up to M 1000
Central Attraction
Tenfold killing of the word Universal History
by ten sharp-shooters of ten German tribes
Souvenirs
Cold Buffet
Rifle range: new kaputt
opposite the dirigible airport
The Festival Committee
of the association for the authorized
shooting of condemned words

This announcement requires an explanation. Fritz Mauthner (1849–1923) was an eminent linguist who published a very learned work entitled *Beiträge zu einer Kritik der Sprache (Contributions to a Critique of Language)* (1901–1903). This title reminds us of Kant's *Critique of Practical Reason*, and the analytical method used is almost identical. Morgenstern read Mauthner's work in December, 1906, that is, after the publication of the first edition of the *Galgenlieder*. He was deeply impressed by the acuteness of Mauthner's reasoning and his brilliant aperçus. He could readily agree with Mauthner's views on the significance of metaphors for the origin of language, but he was strongly opposed to his pragmatism in explaining the evolution of language as a process of decay. According to Mauthner, the visual experience is dissected by the human intellect, and the remains must be digested before a concept and, with it, a word can be born. Language thus becomes a Babylonian tower of decomposed material and can never be used to penetrate the meaning of the universe. Morgenstern's intuitive mind was diametrically opposed to this dissecting method which saw in history an accidental conglomeration of events. For Morgenstern the human personality was a spiritual entity and not an accidental bundle of instincts and sensations. But he earnestly grappled with Mauthner's ideas until he realized their fallacious implications. The above announcement of a Fritz Mauthner Day is a humorous tribute to a false prophet who wants to destroy our faith in the finest product of the human mind: the human language.

A last example of the *Galgenlieder*, "Die zwei Parallelen," shows again the simplicity of its language. As we shall see, the poem points forward, in a wonderful way, to the last two chapters of this study:

> Es gingen zwei Parallelen
> ins Endlose hinaus,
> zwei kerzengerade Seelen
> und aus solidem Haus.
>
> Sie wollten sich nicht schneiden
> bis an ihr seliges Grab:
> das war nun einmal der beiden
> geheimer Stolz und Stab.
>
> Doch als sie zehn Lichtjahre
> gewandert neben sich hin,
> da ward's dem einsamen Paare
> nicht irdisch mehr zu Sinn.
>
> War'n sie noch Parallelen?
> Sie wussten's selber nicht,
> sie flossen nur wie zwei Seelen
> zusammen durch ewiges Licht.
>
> Das ewige Licht durchdrang sie
> da wurden sie eins in ihm;
> die Ewigkeit durchdrang sie
> als wie zwei Seraphim.

Two parallels walked into endless space, two candle-straight souls and from solid stock. They never wanted to meet short of their blessed grave. This was to both their secret pride and guide. When they had wandered ten light years side by side, the lonely pair no longer felt earthly. Were they still parallels? They did not know it themselves. They only flowed together like two souls through endless light. The eternal light pervaded them and they were fused in it. Eternity pervaded them like two Seraphim.

For a moment we are reminded of Heinrich Heine's style which flirts with the simplicity of the folk song. But what a difference there is between the nineteenth-century poet with his skepticism at the threshold of a materialistic era and the twentieth-century herald of a renewed faith in a world of spiritual realities.

CHAPTER 5

Lonely Search for Truth

BEFORE Morgenstern established a widespread reputation through his grotesque poetry, he was well known among the young writers in Berlin as a lyric poet and critic. At that time, Max Reinhardt, the eminent producer of modern and ancient plays and admired innovator of the German stage, was anxious to start a biweekly journal for stagecraft that would stimulate the public's interest in the contemporary stage and in its future. It could be sold with the weekly programs at the Kleines Theater and the Neues Theater in Berlin. Reinhardt suggested Morgenstern as editor. Since his best friend Kayssler was one of the outstanding actors under Reinhardt, Morgenstern was vitally interested in any forward-looking plans in this field. He was opposed to any gross exaggeration, any spectacular stage effects and mechanical devices that could grate on the spectators' nerves. In his view, everything was to reflect the underlying central idea of the play. To be the managing editor of such a controversial journal, with the responsibility of soliciting, accepting, and rejecting contributions of young enthusiasts of all kinds, is a taxing obligation. Morgenstern's physical condition was precarious. As time went on, he felt that his position really required more of a theatrical expert and that he was neglecting his own field. So it was decided that after two years of existence *Das Theater* should suspend publication in the spring of 1905. Morgenstern stayed on as reader for Bruno Cassirer, who had published the journal. Thus Morgenstern's hope to exert a significant influence on Berlin's artistic community faded. Nevertheless, he was aware of the responsibility of his poetic mission. In the poem "Rat und Trost" ("Advice and Consolation") he suggests to his friend that he leave the heavy burden of Atlas behind before entering a bourgeois home: it might frighten the residents, but the children outside would be delighted by the huge resplendent ball (*M*, 123).

The poet sympathizes with those creative minds scattered over the country who languish because the accidents of place and time impede their unfolding. Their sad but unbroken spirits hover over the land like an aura. Although they can only stammer, their ears are attuned to cosmic rhythms. They rise above the dull multitude and venture many a heaven-bound flight from the narrow confines of ordinary existence. From these creative minds will rise the one who takes them unto himself. What does this last line of the poem "Das heimliche Heer" ("The Secret Army") imply (*M*, 102)? It is unlikely that Morgenstern cast himself in the role of an advocate and savior of these frustrated souls, because in the years following the turn of the century his impetuous questions about the meaning of life remained unanswered, as we conclude from his poem "Leben ohne Antwort" (*M*, 110). Morgenstern was constantly searching for the deeper meaning of human existence. This Faustian urge to strive for deeper insights prevented him from becoming complacent. He realized that there is only one place that man can claim as his own: his own self. This is the conclusion reached in the poem "Mensch Wanderer" ("Itinerant Man") (*M*, 101).

Morgenstern's search for his spiritual identity was fundamental to him. It continued for many years, had many aspects, and underwent several changes. It was expressed in verse and prose. According to a poem written in 1901, the solitary hours of reflection were the starting point. They let the poet hear the voices of rare souls ringing in his heart, luring him to lofty heights to fathom with them the meaning of life (*M*, 68). The vast and vague longing for an inner core is mirrored in a poem from 1902:

> Du bist mein Land,
> ich deine Flut,
> die sehnend dich ummeeret;
> du bist der Strand,
> dazu mein Blut
> ohn Ende wiederkehret.

You are my land, I am your sea that longingly embraces you, you are the beach to which my blood unceasingly returns.

The second stanza of the poem speaks of the thousand stars that are reflected on the ocean while the gold of the earth is washed to the bottom of the sea.[1]

Human joys and sorrows find an echo in his heart and unite him with mankind. This we infer from a poem composed in 1904. The evening breeze has wafted a song about wishing and renouncing to the poet, a song that captivated his heart completely. "Was it my longing that came to me as I walked along dreaming?" the poet asks himself, a wondrous song of hopes and tears where the heart struggles with its fate.[2] After spending a few weeks in Wyk on the island of Föhr in the North Sea, Morgenstern felt the need to reinforce his health by a stay in Rantum on the island of Sylt at the end of August, 1905. Instinctively he was preparing for a winter of great spiritual significance. It was like a lull before the big storm. He reports to a friend in Berlin:

I intended to fill my vacation time with a worthwhile spiritual experience and had planned on reading *The Brothers Karamazov* and the memoirs of Prince Kropotkin. But with all the activities in the fresh air, all mental energy dissipates, in the first place, so that I cannot even get up enough willpower to arrange a number of poems dating from the past three years, which would constitute for the public a justification of my existence in the generally accepted manner, although I hardly believe that more than a handful of people ask for such evidence. I myself no longer attach much value to these things. I must confess that this writing of poetry will not be enough for me in the long run. I don't know why the wings won't break through, as it were. They probably are too fragile to cope with reality. At any rate, I am still waiting for myself; I don't accept my present level as a goal.[3]

The poems referred to in this letter were published in 1906 under the title *Melancholie (Melancholia)*.

In these mentally passive but receptive days Morgenstern resigned himself to his fate, which was partly determined by his state of health. At the same time, he had the feeling that great happi-

ness was in store for him. The poem "Sylt—Rantum" expresses his
mood:

> Du abendliche Klarheit dort im Westen,
> sei mir ein Bild von naher Tage Glück.
> Still leg ich mich ins Dünengras zurück
> Nicht wie *ich* will,—wie *es* will, ist's am besten.
>
> (*M*, 118)

You diaphonous light of the evening over there in the West, let it be an
image of the happiness of imminent days. I quietly lie back on the dune
grass. Not the way *I* want, but the way *it* wants is best.

This *amor fati* is an aspect of Morgenstern's pantheistic feeling
which pervaded him at that time and which found expression in at
least two poems. The first of these reminds us of the exuberant
pantheism of the young Goethe in his hymns and certain passages in
Werther when we read how close Morgenstern felt to moss and
grass, realizing that the same forces shaped him and the infinite
world around him. The same warm life pervades everything near
and far away. Man is part of one eternal nature. This poem, consist-
ing of one stanza of twelve lines, was written in 1905 (*M*, 125). The
other one, composed in couplets, is more epigrammatic. The world
is not divided into matter and spirit. Spirit pervades everything. In
the individual the universe becomes aware of itself. Its existence is
its meaning; there is no other purpose. If you call the universe God:

> So bin ich Gott, mit allem was ich bin
> und mein und Gottes ist der gleiche Sinn.
>
> Die Welt ist nicht ein Hier, Gott nicht ein Dort,
> er ist du selbst, wird mit dir fort und fort.
>
> Und nirgends weiss er irgendwie von sich,
> denn als in Wesen so wie du und ich.
>
> (*M*, 124)

Thus I am God with everything I am and mine and God's meaning are the
same. The world is not here, God being there. He is you yourself, is

developing with you, on and on. And nowhere is He aware of Himself in
any way except in beings such as you and I.

In spite of the poet's attempt to bolster his health by spending an
extended vacation on the North Sea islands, his condition compelled
him to avoid Berlin and to stay at a sanitarium in Birkenwerder
some miles outside of the city. We get a glimpse of his state of health
and frame of mind through his vivid description in the first part of
Stufen. Here he writes:

Perhaps this would be the right moment to begin a diary. Outside it has
been raining continuously for nine hours, and this makes me depressingly
aware of my loneliness. This afternoon it flashed through my mind: if I did
not have my work and my thoughts, I couldn't possibly endure such a
patient's life. And I am ill, even if I keep forgetting it and, in the midst of
my illness, have hours, days, weeks, of perfect health, periods of the most
glorious blooming health during which the decay in me is, as it were,
covered up by blossoms, chased away by a spring that knows nothing of fall
and winter of the body, which does violence to the order of nature and
seems to want to save me as an invincible vitality which is resuscitated again
and again. But then a late afternoon with its dangerous idleness would
come, a wet gloomy day like this one and my forgetting of what is is a thing
of the past. I see him before me, my most faithful companion and pursuer,
the strangest creature in the world. His occupation for ten, fourteen years
has been to tickle me in my windpipe with a light feather as if there were
nothing in the world that he would rather do than hear my voice again and
again, hour after hour, day after day, year after year, merely my voice,
inarticulate without form, without contents, while he himself may be
merely a beastly ghost, a brainless demon, nothing but a fixed idea from top
to bottom, and I his only target, his only purpose in life. (S, 27)

In this situation Morgenstern must have had an additional urgent
incentive to lose himself in his pursuit of ultimate insights. The
ideas he had expressed in his pantheistic poems provided food for
further meditations which were published after his death under the
heading "Tagebuch eines Mystikers" "Diary of a Mystic". They con-
stitute a highlight of *Stufen* and begin with these words: "I wrote
this at the point where man coincides with God, where he ceases to
experience himself as a separate being." Then Morgenstern defines

religion as he saw it at that point: "Religion is the realization that all thinking is God's thinking, just as all nature is God's nature, that every action is an action by God, every thought a thought of God, that God is God only in as far as He is the world, that the world is nothing but God Himself, that in the moment when a human being becomes aware of his being, God in him becomes aware of Himself as man" (S, 222).

Gradually Morgenstern realized the unheard-of consequences of his new insight into the mystic unity of God and man for everyday life. He describes himself sitting in a café: "From one's marbletop table behind one's cup to watch those who come and go, who sit down and engage in conversation, and to see through the huge window those outside, moving here and there like swarming fish behind the glass wall of a large container, and now and then to indulge in the idea: this is you! And to see them all, how they do not know who they are, who speaks to Himself in their guise and who recognizes them through my eyes as Himself and from theirs only as people (S, 228). Pursuing the same trend of thought, Morgenstern describes the tradition-bound members of the so-called good society, more or less amiable people who believe that they can settle down at the age of thirty. "They are predictable, and yet they have the most unpredictable thing inside, a soul that is capable of doing any outrageous deed. They have entirely forgotten or never comprehended that they are—God. They are satisfied to be Mr. X or Mrs. Y and to live and die only as such (S, 227).

The idea of the identity of God and man shed a new light on the role of evil and suffering among human beings. Referring to Dostoevski's *The Brothers Karamazov*, Morgenstern observes:

Ivan Karamazov rejects this world. Even if he could understand everything, he cannot understand the suffering of children. But what if all this suffering is, in the last analysis, self-inflicted, God's own suffering. Suppose all mankind and any conceivable mankind of the universe is God Himself, the immeasurably great, terrible, tragic life of God Himself! Only one second of a vague inkling of himself as God Himself in a person's brain, would it not resolve everything, not in inexpressible harmony—oh no—but in an abyss, never to be grasped and felt, of such error and depth that any accusation, any complaint, even any judgment would be silenced. (S, 229)

In a later passage, Morgenstern ponders the relationship of God and man: "I believe that this shadowy self-awareness of God in man is, at the same time, his only self-awareness. God is imprisoned in nature, if we may say so. God wrests Himself out of it to become the spirit that recognizes Himself. Man is God's head. But, just like man, God will never attain real self-awareness (getting only an inkling of it), for He has cognition only to the extent that He is man" (S, 230).

Morgenstern could not help but carry his religious speculations over into his reading. After perusing a French novel, possibly as a reader for Cassirer, he wrote:

Look at this love of two people who are spared the ordinary cares of everyday life—this, if you wish, criminal love because it is carried on secretly and illicitly. Look at these two creatures of luxury whom the proletarian would strangle if he were to invade the bourgeois homes once more. Imagine close by, hardly a block away, stark misery, crippling disease, filth, villainy, and crime, and ask yourself what a God would have to do were he not identical with it. Only a world that is God Himself can be as it is. God spares Himself nothing. He is the love of those refined, daring creatures of luxury. He is their ecstasy. . . . He is this love Himself, just as He is the misery, disease, the filth. He does not need to blush like a cheap hedonist. He is not the thief of another person's property. He does not obtain his ecstasies in devious ways. In a terrifying abundance and truth, He is everything from top to bottom. He is the whole universe in His own body; to say it once again: He is allowed to be everything because He *is* everything. (S, 231)

A natural extension of this idea is found in another entry in the diary: "The one and only command is: You are allowed to do everything you want to do, but keep in mind that you are doing it yourself" (S, 223).

Morgenstern's evolutionary pantheism could not accept a shallow optimism based solely on the progress of modern science. "With this *Zählmaschine* ["computer"] in his hand man becomes an occupied and quiet school child. The awesomeness of existence loses its sway over him, he classifies, clarifies, corrects here and there. A world for which there is only one designation, terrifying, finally becomes for him a comfortable residence into which death casts an uncomfortable shadow. Death, thanks a million times that you are the ineradicable ingredient of our lives. Without you the whole endeavor of every thinking person would have to be directed to this end: to invent you. Without you, God would be rotting in His own body" (S, 232).

When we remember that Morgenstern wrote the "Diary of a Mystic" at a sanitarium in Birkenwerder, we can understand his interest in the problem of death. Thus he meditates on its inevitability: "My death as an individual is my confirmation as part of the world. For my death as such is necessary to the life of the whole, and since I myself am a part as well as the whole, my death is necessary for myself" (S, 225). Taking his own death as a challenge, he expresses his conviction:

I shall not die until I have accomplished what I am able to accomplish. God does not die prematurely. He awakes here and goes to sleep there, wherever it is "meet and right." Why do you resist what you call your fate? Look yourself in the eye. Your fate is that you are God. I say God! But if the realization of this word should dawn on us, then our heart and brain would be annihilated like Bologna glass which, when shattered, disintegrates into dust. The ancient peoples knew that to see God means death, and that to divine God means life. (S, 225)

How much rationalizing is contained in this line of reasoning? we may ask when we look at another passage from the biographical part of the Stufen, not contained in the mystic diary. The knowledge that he did not have many years to live prompted the poet to remark: "It is bitter to have to accomplish between thirty-five and forty-five what you should have been able to accomplish between forty-five and sixty" (S, 26). Morgenstern died at the age of forty-three.

Sensitive as he was, he felt, at times, that the urgency of his mission might have made him too impatient toward others. Among his epigrams of 1906 we find the following: "Verzeiht mir, bin ich schroff und hart, / doch kurz ist meine Gegenwart" ("Forgive me, if I am abrupt and harsh, but my presence is limited"); "Wer in den Tod tut marschieren, / der lernt leicht Soldatenmanieren" ("He who marches into death, is likely to adopt a soldier's manners"). On the other hand, his readiness to die is expressed in this epigram: "O Tod, so nimm denn dies mein Leben hin! / Dein Sinn ist tief; dein

Sinn ist stets Mein Sinn."[4] ("Oh death, take this my life. Your meaning is profound; your meaning is always my meaning").

In the preceding discussion of Morgenstern's mysticism, we have disregarded his relationship to the Christian faith. Yet it is a very important element of his religion. In the "Autobiographical Note," which serves as an introduction to the *Stufen,* we find the following description of the religious breakthrough of 1906: "Meanwhile the thirty-five-year-old had a crucial experience. Nature and man had become for him spiritual manifestations. And when one evening he opened once again the Gospel according to St. John, he believed that he had come to an actual understanding for the first time" (S, 12). What Morgenstern means here becomes evident in the self-portrait which he presents in his "Diary of a Mystic":

Imagine the most ordinary man in the world with a vivid imagination, easily aroused and tenacious, with some poetic talent, without exceptional character traits, but prompted by the constant wish to become more spiritual . . . with an inborn cheerfulness of mind, with a certain inclination toward mockery and lassitude, widely read without any expert training, having a poor memory, unskilled and slow in dialectics, thorough only in his persistence always to pursue, consciously or unconsciously, only this one goal: to recognize himself within the framework of the outside world. Imagine such a person one day understanding the word: I and the Father are one. Imagine how his mind revolves around this word, or rather how he lets this word revolve within him, for he does not pounce upon his inner experiences, but lets them live or die in accordance with their own strength. How this strength seems to bring about an ultimate awareness of himself, as if everything else would be blindness, as if it were a derangement to feel himself, in regard to God, as something different, adjacent, coordinate, or even subordinate, to discuss the problem of God at all in any way, as if one had to prove one's own existence. "You are all in me, but in whom am I?—He who has me has the Father." How these constant repetitions used to vex me, how simple and obstinate they appeared to me, as if a child were repeating the same thing over and over again. Until one evening it dawned on me from what feeling this tireless emphasis must have emanated. (S, 223)

Morgenstern's evolutionary pantheism was a natural result of his way of experiencing of the world. In his "Diary of a Mystic" he states:

My highest idea has nothing to do with the external course of my life. I am not one of those who have been impelled to the resumption of the idea of God through some external fact such as suppressed sensuality, loneliness of the soul, despairing of oneself and of the world, or the like. I know these mental conditions but I would never have fled from them into a new concept of God. The latter will neither "heal" nor "redeem." Rather this idea is an outgrowth of my innermost nature. I can trace its beginnings back to the second decade of my life, when, at its midpoint, a very specific philosophical interest awakened in me. Its eventual breakthrough is very much connected with my way of viewing things which allows me, at times, to be immersed in the things, thus to make my identifying myself with everything a natural reaction. (S, 250)

In another passage of the diary, Morgenstern makes the historical statement: "In Christ God has attained an awareness of Himself for the first time on earth. In Christ God becomes aware of Himself as a human being for the first time" (S, 251). Thus the poet comes to his own interpretation of the dogma of the Trinity. "Centuries have quarreled about the word Trinity. And yet it comprises the world interpreted for a child. The Father is life which is all-inclusive and which the individual person can never grasp, let alone explain intellectually. The Son is the same divine life, as a divining being, as a human being, as Christ—as the human being in particular. The Holy Ghost, this is the slow fermenting progress of the realization, on earth, that God is everything" (S, 226).

As I have previously stated, Morgenstern sees the universe identified with God, having many levels of consciousness and reaching His highest self-awareness in the most spiritual human being on earth. But in one passage this unified picture is extended into cosmic space. This idea is not alien to Christian theology. Klopstock's poetry touches on this aspect. Morgenstern, however, is more specific. He states in his "Diary of a Mystic":

We must refrain from thinking exclusively of the human race on our planet. We must assume that any possible thought concerning God is actually thought by God, whether it is in our minds or in those dwelling on Mars or Saturn, that planets may very well exist on which God lives, as it were, bodily in complete awareness of Himself. We assume that, as the phase of God we are, we evidently merely represent God in one phase, not necessarily in His highest, although His highest phase could well be a finite one while the infinite mystery can remain infinite only in a continuous finite form. God can live by way of His continual death. God must die continually in order to live everlastingly. (S, 244)

In Morgenstern's letters written during this critical period, we note that he was reluctant to speak about his spiritual breakthrough except in the most general terms. In July 1906, he does mention the "Diary of a Mystic" as a natural climax of an autobiographical novel which he had planned to write, but after five months he felt that he was still too close to the experience to speak about it. In September he disclosed to Fritz Kayssler: "Last January or February an overwhelming idea dawned on me, not as a sudden revelation but as a climax of my previous inner development, and the entire rest of my life and artistic endeavor will probably have to serve to this end to fathom this idea" (B, September 14, 1906). In October he reported that he was still thinking of his novel but that the very unstable condition of his health prevented him from accomplishing any large project. In fact, Morgenstern never completed the novel, fragments of which were published in *Stufen*. The restricted life he was leading in the sanitarium in Birkenwerder permitted him to do extensive reading. In the writings of Meister Eckhart, the fourteenth-century German mystic, he found confirmation of his own mystic thought. The Russian people appealed to him especially during this period. He admired the novelist in Tolstoy, but the latter's religious views, which made him denounce all modern art as degenerate, found no support in Morgenstern. He was greatly impressed by the Moscow theater that had come to Berlin for four weeks. The Russians somehow conveyed the impression of a more mature humanity. Their love of life was more intense than that of the Germans or the French. There was also an unspoken feeling of love for each other that was taken for granted. Morgenstern felt that the future of mankind was with the Russians rather than with the Americans. Dostoevski was, for him, the outstanding Russian writer. He likens him to the prairie fire that wends its smoldering way through the tall grass until, fanned by a storm, it flares up to the clouds, illuminating heaven and earth with its brilliance. In the diary we read: "If I were a priest I would touch the ground before him with my forehead three times before turning to my brothers and speaking to them. For in him one of the great lights of the earth that shine in the darkest nights came alive" (S, 236). In another passage Morgenstern describes how Dostoevski first arouses our interest in his figures, who are faced with all kinds of complications until the hour comes for each of them to reveal their innermost feelings. Their chief concern are religious questions: Is there a God? What must we do if there is not; and are the Russian people the only nation that supports God? In these conversations the flame of God is burning and struggling for His identity, whose body is the infinite universe of stars and whose spirit is the spirit of all living things (S, 235). Thus Morgenstern projected his pantheism into the work of Dostoevski, whom he considered as one of the great modern leaders along with Lagarde and Nietzsche.

In July, 1906, Morgenstern journeyed to Tirol, in the hope that the thinner mountain air would bring relief to his lungs. Since life in the summer resort Längenfeld did not provide the rest and quiet he needed, the poet moved to Obergurgl, a small village in a narrow valley at the foot of snow-capped mountains. In early September he traveled to Obermais near Merano where he found a small but neat room in the Villa Kirchlechner. His balcony offered a splendid view of the mountains and over the valley. Both the landscape and the solicitous motherly landlady made him feel at home there. He spent the winter in semiseclusion, writing and devoting a good deal of time to reading philosophy: Fichte, Hegel, Böhme, and especially Spinoza. In these he found confirmation of his own views. In the spring of 1907 he took a trip to Lake Garda and then traveled north to Switzerland, where he stayed in the neighborhood of Lucerne, later in Wolfenschiessen and Tenigerbad, located in a high wooded valley. His hermitlike existence appealed to him.

Now that the division between the physical world and the world of the spirit no longer existed for Morgenstern he could see the one reflected in the other. An inner experience could well be represented by an external situation. The feeling of being on the brink of death, when the longing for eternity and the natural shrinking back from it becomes an acute struggle, could well be pictured by mountain scenery. That is what we find in the second and third poems in the collection of lyrics entitled *Einkehr (Introspection)* published in 1910:

> Raumschwindelgefühl
> Euch engen Berge ein—
> Mir zeigt ihr scharfer Saum
> nur umso grausiger
> den grenzlosen Raum.
>
> Wie einer Schleuder Kelch
> den flugbereiten Stein,
> so engt mich des Gebirgs
> verwünschter Sattel ein.

Space dizziness: mountains hem you in—their sharp edge all the more gruesomely shows me the boundless space. Just as the cup of a sling restrains the stone poised for flight, so does the unwelcome crest of the mountain restrain me.

In response to this longing for eternity, mortal man shrinks from the imminent plunge.

> Notschrei
>
> . . . lass dich Berg mein Elend jammern!
> Meines Geists entschwerte Flügel
> reissen mich aus deinen Toren
> in den Raum hinaus—und zeigen
> mir den Ball in grausem Schweigen
> im Unendlichen verloren. . . .

Cry for help: mountain, take pity on my plight. The weightless wings of my spirit hurl me out of your gates into space and show me the globe in uncanny silence lost in the boundless realm.

The realization of the precariousness of his health could not help but produce in the poet an undercurrent of anticipation of an early departure, reflected not only in his letters but also, now and then, in his poetry. The evening hours inspire a kindred mood. The poet's

glance rests on the immense azure above him and then roams back
to the familiar earth as confidence alternates with anxiety. When the
warm light of the evening spreads its radiance over woods and
meadows, his heart which, he believes, has invited eternity too
early goes out to them (M, 152). Assured, as he is, of his spiritual
self, the poet cannot bring himself to leave this beautiful earth of
ours. This experience is expressed in the famous lines from *Einkehr:*

> O bunte Welt,
> was schillerst du mir her!
> Auf mich gestellt,
> bedarf ich dein nicht mehr.
>
> Nicht mehr? Und doch
> Wie bangt mich oft nach dir . . .
> zu innig noch
> verschlingt sich Dort und Hier.

Oh, brightly colored world, why should you lure me, relying on myself. I
need you no more. No more? And yet how often I long for you. Too closely
this life and that beyond are entwined.

The same motif runs through a number of poems composed in the
wake of Morgenstern's spiritual breakthrough of 1906. At night the
temptation to leave this earth seems to be greater. So the poet is
grateful when the light of the sun does not leave him. When the
snow-white quivering rays of the full moon reflect the sun's light to
him he responds in gratitude to the everlasting love that pursues the
earth even when it turns away from the sun (M, 154). With his gaze
fixed at the firmament, the poet is comforted by the murmur of the
mountain spring behind him which reminds him that earth's nature
surrounds him and protects him against the temptation of the spirit
that might lure him into a bottomless abyss.[5] Awareness that this
earth of ours is floating in the boundless space could make the poet
dizzy, but he is reassured by a hundred familiar pictures inspiring
trust. His awe is tempered into shy reverence, and he gratefully
seeks the earth's protective sphere (M, 161). Finally, we turn to the
poem in *Einkehr* called "Versuchung" ("Temptation"). In substance

it is reminiscent of Christ's temptation by the devil; in point of view it reminds us of Rilke's idea of death that ripens in the human soul. The voice of temptation in the poet's mind urges him to take the plunge into the abyss since he is, after all, immortal. It only takes a determined "I want to." You yourself said, the voice whispers, that God goes to sleep here and wakes up there. Well then—go to sleep. You will not cease to exist, even for a moment; for what you give up is merely your bodily shape. Then comes the poet's answer:

> Mein Tagwerk ist noch nicht vollbracht.
> Wer an der Schale sich vergreift,
> bevor sie ihren Kern gereift,—
> er schläft zu früh ein—und erwacht—
> zu spät.

My day's work is not yet finished. He who destroys the shell before the core is ripe goes to sleep too early—and awakens too late.

Suicide impedes the evolution of the spiritual self in the other world in the progression from one reincarnation to the next. The latter interpretation seems possible when we keep in mind that Morgenstern studied the life and teaching of Buddha early in 1908, reinforcing the idea of reincarnation which the poet expressed in several of his earliest printed poems. The temptation to reach beyond the confines of our five senses can likewise be traced back to Morgenstern's high school days. In *Stufen* we find the following description:

As a high school senior I attempted for the first time to have a living experience of what we call the boundlessness of the universe. I lay down at night on a folding chair in the garden in an almost horizontal position and tried hard to penetrate through what I could see of the starlit sky into its reality. I succeeded so well that I felt: one more second of such physical detachment, one more tiny step, and my senses will leave me forever. And I broke off the weird experiment. Now, about fifteen years later, the same danger is threatening me in broad daylight. It started on a steel-blue spring evening in a park in Obermais with the view of the range of mountains bordering on the Vinschgau. The mountains took on the dimensions of a molehill, and the village and the surrounding countryside lost their significance. The valley appeared as small as the imprint of a thumb on a wax ball, and the huge yet small planet carried me like a gnat on its back through space. A slight mental dizziness, a presentiment of a seasickness of the mind seized me. The concepts of top and bottom were fused. I was sitting there by the grace of air pressure. (S, 30).

The above poems included in *Einkehr* are characterized by their cosmic awareness and their religious overtones. This applies also to "Abendweise" ("Evening Melody"). Here we may think of the Teutonic forebears who worshiped in sacred groves where they presented their offerings; the poet shows us night as such a sacred grove where our reverent thoughts rise heavenward in a quiet, steady flame. "Mondnacht" ("Moonlit Night") paints an Alpine scene at night with black hills in front and, back of them, the steep rocky walls rising in the light of the moon as if behind a haze woven by spirits. Is it not, asks the poet, an image of earthbound gloom and heavenly striving: the lower regions are still filled with darkness, but above them there is soulful light. Unforgettable is the impression of the inexorable seriousness of the poem which closes the first part of *Einkehr* entitled "Im Hochgebirge" ("In the High Mountains"). As we read this poem, "Vor Sonnenaufgang" ("Before Sunrise"), we may keep in mind that the hours before sunrise are the most critical for the moribund (Morgenstern died at 4:30 A.M.) and that the often inaccessible woods high up in the Alps are a very lonely place, an outpost of the universe. The ravens, harbingers of doom, link this poem with the songs of the gallows, but the contrast is unmistakable.

> Raben halten wo im Alpenwald Gericht. . . .
>
> Durch den Raum hin schwebt im Morgenlicht
> geisterleis der mütterliche Ball. . . .
>
> Raben schrein im geisterstummen All. . . .

Ravens preside over a court of justice somewhere in the Alpine woods. In the light of early morning the motherly globe glides through space in ghostlike whisper. Ravens screech in the universe while the spirits are silenced.

CHAPTER 6

Companionship for Life

THE year 1908 was destined to bring great personal happiness to Morgenstern, but it did not start very auspiciously. His father, Carl Ernst, who had shut his son out of his life, had seen some stormy years and was now anxious to effect a reconciliation with Christian. The latter was willing to meet him halfway if the older man really had a change of heart. Carl's third wife, Elisabeth, had been quite prejudiced against Christian because she believed that he had opposed his father's third marriage. In reply to the first letter from his parents, Christian told them that a few kind words could not make up for all the years of indifference toward him, and that he was no longer the young student whom his father had neglected and rejected. The traditional father-son relationship would have to be supplemented by a new relationship of mutual affection and trust which could not spring up from one day to the next, but needed to be nurtured with sincere goodwill. This might take a good deal of time and effort. The result of this letter was a great disappointment on the part of the father and an attempt, on the part of Elisabeth, to make him an ally against her husband. In order to win him over, she indulged in such fantasies as to nurse him back to health. Christian hoped to effect a rapprochement by telling both parents about his work as a poet and translator of Ibsen. But now a further complication arose when Professor Morgenstern expected his son to break off the friendly relationship with his former stepmother. Christian did not want to take sides, since he felt sorry for Amélie, his father's second wife, who had become lonely and confused after the divorce. The attempt to isolate Amélie was probably initiated by Elisabeth.

In his reply, Christian became quite frank in assessing the situation. He had been abandoned by his family. "When my father was

89

twenty-three years old, my grandfather showed him the world, when his son was twenty-three years old, the door of his home was shut behind him as behind a dead person. And he would probably have gone downhill and died if he had not been loved by one person, the only one who can and should use the word loyal in relationship to him" (*B*, February 24, 1908), Christian writes in his letter to Elisabeth, referring to Fritz Kayssler. It was very painful for this loyal friend to see how the older Morgenstern and his wife underestimated the poet's immaculate character and his entirely unselfish motives in trying to establish an atmosphere of absolute frankness and goodwill rising above all petty jealousy and juggling for psychological advantages. He realized that his father unwittingly did his son the greatest favor by banishing him from his influence. How much emotional friction Christian had thus been spared during the significant years of his development! Father and son lived in two different worlds. Success, fame, and the good life were at the top of the scale of social values for Carl Ernst; not so for Christian, who had to struggle for his economic survival. Repeatedly he thought of joining an organization that would insure shelter and a hospital bed in case of emergency. Apparently it never occurred to the father, who was quite well off, to inquire about his son's economic situation, and the latter was, of course, too proud to raise the subject.

Unfortunately, subsequent letters from Elisabeth revealed her to be somewhat less than forthright. In June and July, 1908, Christian stayed at a sanitarium in Schlachtensee near Berlin. There a brief reconciliation between father and son took place. A year later, Christian visited the home of his parents in Wolfshau, Silesia. By avoiding all serious conversation, the three managed to spend a few harmonious days together. After Elisabeth's death, Christian complied with his father's wish and renounced all claims to the Wolfshau home, so it could be left to the city of Breslau to provide a home for indigent artists in need of rest and recuperation. This pledge was redeemed after the father's death by establishing the "Carl and Elisabeth Morgenstern Endowment." In the light of this public generosity, it is ironic that during his son's last years the older Morgenstern never wondered whether he could extend any financial help to his ailing son.

In the years following his spiritual breakthrough, the poet lived a rather hermitlike existence, partly imposed upon him by his delicate health, and partly in accordance with his own wishes. He did not want to be distracted by the hustle and bustle of everyday life. We can easily understand his mood, expressed in the poem "Einsiedlerwunsch" ("A Hermit's Wish"). Here he wishes for a hut and a piece of land in the woods. He believes that he will soon be forgotten among his fellowmen; then his life and his work might become significant and he would soon forget time in search of God (*M*, 164). This is why the conflict with his parents was so distressing to him that it almost made him ill. In "Schlussgespräch mit mir selbst" ("Final Conversation with Myself"), he admonishes himself to exercise strict self-discipline. He thinks of the pearl and the jewel whose origin is pain and pressure. He thinks of the inner realm, of the man from Galilee, and how he broke up the world to establish his inner kingdom. And yet this kingdom is the whole universe. And now the poet doubted whether he was taking his pantheism seriously enough. He did not yet feel truly an integral part of the universe:"Noch ist dein Meer mir nicht der Meere Meer / Noch bin ich Wind, den keine Rast bestieht" (*M*, 142) ("Your ocean is not yet the ocean of oceans for me. I am still the wind that cannot be enticed by any calm"). Instead of being a drop in the ocean, he is still an *isola* ("island") and this isolation makes him unsightly in the sight of God. Thus in the poem "Ich und der Vater sind eins" ("I and the Father are One") the poet admonishes himself:

> Tu ab die Fremdheit, die dich hässlich macht!
> Das Schaffen deines Gottes, der du selbst,
> lieb es voll Schmerz und Seligkeit, wo irgend
> du sein gewahrst!
> . . . und schönres Wort vielleicht
> fand nie ein Mensch für sich,
> den dreimal Unbegreiflichen,
> als da er, ratlos anders sich zu nennen,
> sich Sohn und Vater nannte—
> und in Christus sprach:
> Ich und der Vater—
> sind Eins.[1]

Cast off the isolation that makes you unsightly, the creative work of God, love it, filled with pain and happiness, wherever you become aware of it. . . . And perhaps never did a human being find a more beautiful word for himself, the thrice incomprehensible one, than when, at a loss to call himself otherwise, he called himself son and father ans spoke through Christ: I and the Father are One.

This pantheism, which finds its key in Christ's awareness of His unity with God, is persistently expressed in Morgenstern's poetry. In "Das Kornfeld" ("The Wheatfield"), the poet observes a wheatfield swaying in the breeze and imagines each ear to be endowed with a soul and a spirit. Standing at the edge of a glacier, where, through the geological shift, the rock foundation is laid bare, Morgenstern touches the rock with his human hand: "I used to sleep just like you, didn't I?" the poet asks in "Gletscherschliff" ("Edge of the Glacier") "immobile and insensible, biding my distant time in majestic repose, and now I stand, a late fruit, a remarkable prize running my hand over the formation of strange runes" (*M*, 161). To appreciate Morgenstern's cosmic sweep from the consciousness of the rock to the skull of man we must add a poem from *Einkehr* entitled "Die Wunderfrucht" ("The Miracle Fruit"), which says: "My temples rest in my right hand, like a fruit clasped in my fingers. If anyone could grasp what is going on in this miracle fruit, in the most delicate cells, inside this hard warm shell, this meditating fruit! My hand clasps the sacred vault, from whose unexplored sanctuary there wells up the glory of individual feeling, the radiance that has become aware of itself as spirit, God's dawning awareness of himself, like a huge nut."[2]

"Memento," the short form of *memento mori* ("think of death"), takes on a new meaning in Morgenstern's pantheism. Nature reminds him, rightly so, of the frailty of the human body. He is running a race with the steady pace of fate. Sometimes he seems to have gained on fate, but eventually they will arrive together at the little place called *Totenbrück* ("bridge of death"). Suddenly the poet stops and flings the pagan word "fate" into the face of his own time. He recalls his identity with God and is intent on his goals, moving through a thousand darknesses, decreeing life and death for himself

(*M*, 177). In the same vein, the following triumphant epigram is written:

> Den Kelch der Ewigkeit am Munde
> was sorgst du der verlornen Stunde!
> Empfandst du nur ein einzig Mal: Ich Bin:—
> So gibst du stumm wohl auch ein Leben hin.[3]

Eternity's cup is at your lips, why should you worry about a wasted hour. If you felt the I Am even a single time you will give up your life without a murmur.

Einkehr closes with an elaboration of John 14:6:

> Ich bin der Weg, die Wahrheit und das Leben,
> niemand kommt zum Vater denn durch mich.
> Ihr mögt nach allen Winden streben—
> wer flöhe Sich?
> Sich aber sah nur einer: ich.
> Mich fassend, mich in Geist und Wahrheit mich,
> wirst du der Finsternis entschweben.
> O fass mich doch! O lass mich dich erheben!
> Ich liebe dich.

I am the way, and the truth, and the life, no one comes to the Father, but through me. You stray in all directions—who could ever escape Himself. But only one saw Himself, I. Grasping Me, in spirit and truth grasping Me, you will soar above the darkness. Do grasp Me, do. Do let Me lift you up. I love you.

This is the last of five fragments from an uncompleted lyrical cycle on Christ. It is important to note that this cornerstone of Morgenstern's Christ-oriented pantheism was already developed before the poet met Margareta Gosebruch von Liechtenstern, his future wife.

Morgenstern was willing to accept what life offered him and did not complain about sickness and poverty. But one thing weighed on his mind: that fate did not let him find the noble type of woman he dreamed of: a true comrade, a free soul, a graceful body. As late as 1907, he expressed the following somewhat drastic views:

Dance of death is no theme at all. They should draw and paint how the woman pulls the man into the big hotchpotch. At the bottom: the vast triviality of contemporary life, and leading into this paltriness an endless chain of woman and man, the woman always ahead with a thousand gestures from the most innocent to the most lascivious. The men who are of any account want to work; they want to move the world forward, but the woman wants, more than anything, to settle down. The present satisfies her completely, and she feels fully justified if she serves the future by producing children. In spite of the inconvenience, it is the easiest way to promote the progress of mankind. One presents a child, that is, one restricts oneself to pass on one's task, to supply a third party. As long as the women have not comprehended the fact that outside of their usual domestic ideal there might be other, greater cultural ideals, mankind will not advance significantly. That is why I am so fond of the Russians and Scandinavians, for there one is most likely to find women who are not thinking only of themselves but also of their husbands, who really support them as comrades and not as legal concubines who merely want to make them the top slaves in the household. (S, 186)

Hence it would not have been enough for Morgenstern to have a devoted, loving wife willing to share his outwardly insecure life and to follow him everywhere. She would have to have the kind of mind which, on its own accord, could fully share his spiritual views and possibly even lead him on in the direction he was going.

It was in Dreikirchen in southern Tirol that this instinctive longing found fulfillment beyond his fondest hopes. Morgenstern had found this small summer resort among wood-clad hills at the foot of the Alps through a travel guide, in fact through the same guidebook that had induced Margareta and her companion, a Russian baroness, to spend their month's vacation there. The poet usually had an aversion to eating with the other guests whom chance would bring together at the boardinghouse table. This time, however, it was different. Christian's and Margareta's mutual attraction grew steadily as they spent several hours together day after day, at mealtime, taking hikes, playing chess, and engaging in long conversations. As his love for the young lady took hold of him more and more firmly, he could not escape the disturbing thought that he was no longer exclusively committed to what he felt was his poetic mission in life. He had imposed monastic rules on himself which would exclude marriage. But as it turned out, this love did not distract him from his poetry; it rather increased his productivity in a wonderful way. The blissful feeling of being loved in return, however reservedly, opened the poetic well in him. In *Mensch Wanderer* we find this sonnet:

> Ich habe nicht gewusst, dass so viel Liebe
> in einem Herzen sein kann—und zu mir.
> Zwar—ich bin ungerecht. Und doch . . . es hat
> mich nimmermehr zuvor so überwältigt.
>
> So will ich sagen: Wissen um die Liebe,
> das tat ich stets, und war auch wohl zu Gast,—
> wo wie ein Gast von Wein und Herdglut weiss,
> Durch Dich erst aber *glaub* ich an die Liebe.
>
> Selbst (und das ist das schwerste) an die meine:
> an meine Fähigkeit zu jener letzten
> Vereinigung des ewig sonst Ent-zweiten.
>
> Nun nicht mehr Gast nur wandl' ich durch die Zeiten—
> nun sitz ich selbst am Herd und atme Frieden,
> und glaub an alle Liebe—durch die Deine.

I did not know that so much love can be in one heart—and for me. Although—I am unjust. And yet . . . it has never overwhelmed me so strongly before. So I would say: know about love I always did, and was also invited, I suppose,—just as a guest knows about home and the glow of the hearth. But only through you I believe in love, even (and that is the hardest) in mine, in my ability for the ultimate union of what was otherwise divided forever. Now no longer a guest, I move through the temporal sphere,—now I am sitting at the hearth myself, enjoying peace and believing in all—through yours.

At the end of August, the two young ladies had to leave their vacation spot. How hard it was for Christian and Margareta to part is illustrated by the fact that they walked the two hours from Dreikirchen to the railway station Waidbruck only to decide to take the train to a distant hill, and from there to climb to the Penegal peak the next day. Thus they spent two more very happy days together,

at the end of which the poet escorted the two young ladies to Bol-
zano. We have a poem entitled "Die dritte erzählt" ("The Third
Party Relates") in which Margareta's girl friend relates, for the poet,
the moods of the last minutes before parting:

It was at the time when no word of love had yet been spoken. I sat between
you and her as we were waiting for the train from the valley. Something had
cast a silence filled with sadness upon you. I felt a wave of love and sorrow
and longing surge through me who separated the two of you. Forgive me
that I remained between you and let you seek each other and embrace and
kiss each other through me. The heavy evening clouds, carried by the south
wind, sailed in the pale sky on the edge of the mountains we had just left,
like a second spectral range—a fate painful but also great. In them there was
the gesture of the great nameless heartache called life.

No sooner was Morgenstern back in Obermais than he wrote a long
letter to Margareta:

I am sitting here in the garden of the restaurant on the Fountain Square as
the only guest, thinking, thinking of you, and I must tell you that. For even
if the last week or two don't lead to what the people commonly imagine they
would, I did love you in these days and I feel that you are woven into my life
as an integral and indispensable part. I must write this to you, and I permit
myself to do so, for after all is said and done, I am not one who brings grief. I
realize that with my confession—which you must often have read in my
eyes before (I was always afraid to lose my eyes in yours, as you were afraid
of losing yours in mine) I am shouldering a responsibility and yet I know, at
the same time, that you will emerge from this strange experience safe and
strong. You will not be harmed in anything, not in your dear young body
nor in your dear young soul which you know so well to hide so austerely and
demurely without being able to conceal its sweetness and excitability from a
person like me. Yes—this has touched me most about you, this unchanging
kindness which you showed me from the outset, this doing without all the
things with which women can torture one. You must not speak of such
kindness on my part. I have sometimes taken advantage of your affection. I
have hurt you sometimes, not willfully, because I did not feel as sensitively,
not quite the same way as you do. Do not think that I never noticed it. I did,
and I ask you to forgive me. . . . (B, August 31, 1908)

Each of the subsequent days, Morgenstern wrote long letters to

Margareta, sometimes even more than one. Among other things, we learn how productive the poet had become through her. The smallest stimulation fell on fertile ground and began to germinate, to his own amazement. Some verses appeared in finished form and remained unchanged, others were not yet what they could have been. Poems on nature are superfluous, he said, unless they show utmost conciseness. Many happy ideas came to him and many were lost again as he hiked in the gloriously refreshing air on the roads near Merano and Obermais. After ten days he realized that he could not continue this daily correspondence to the same extent, and he confessed his irregular working habits. When the spirit came over him he was happy and did not think of the next day. Deserted by the spirit, he felt ill at ease and did not know where to turn. Many people of this type would reach for a tranquillizer, but for health reasons, he could not even resort to smoking. A few days later, he suggested to Margareta to read portions of *Zarathustra* from which he could still draw strength and comfort. Meanwhile he had received a letter from Margareta, and he now asked her not to worry about his health. He was convinced that it would hold up, at least, until he had attained the maturity of which he was capable. Margareta's inquiry about his views on predestination he answered in the light of his evolutionary pantheism. The letter of September 23 contains his poem "The Two Parallels" which was quoted at the end of Chapter 4.

In the letter of October 8, the poet speaks of his profound seriousness, his courage and resoluteness in spiritual matters. His creative will and her ingenious receptiveness together should protect them from being compared to other couples. If Margareta should happen to be his whole love, to the depth he imagines it to be, then she would indeed be his first and last love. What he had experienced before was a need for tenderness, his admiration for gracefulness, and never passion. His problem now was whether he was capable of the great passion, not just of being passionate. He was grateful to his destiny that he once saw Margareta hurry to one of the little churches for prayer, probably in her anxiety over her girl friend. That is when he realized her deeper self. He implores the powers of fate:

Ihr ewigen Mächte, denen ich verbunden bin,
ihr wart mir immer gut. Verlasst mich nicht auch nun
in Diesem. Denn ich bin nicht stark genug allein.

Zerbrecht dies Herz, ihr kennt's, das Liebe nie zerbrach,
nie zerbrach so, dass all sein Eis hinschmolz, hinfloss:
helft mir's zerbrechen, und—zerbräch ich selbst mit ihm.

(M, 187)

Eternal powers to whom I am devoted. You have always been kind to me.
Don't forsake me now in this. For I am not strong enough by myself. Break
this heart in two which you know, which has never been broken, so that all
its ice melted away, floated away: help me break it in two, even if I were to
be broken with it.

On October 15, Morgenstern realized that he had provoked a
crisis in Margareta. Her mother, a general's widow, objected to
her relationship with a poet. The latter felt that he had to see her to
discuss the various difficulties and possibilities. He must keep Margareta from becoming ill. His self-analysis must cease, and so it will
as soon as he can read in her eyes, for never before has a woman
looked at him with real love. On October 18, Morgenstern told
Margareta that he considered her to be the one who had been
reserved for him, as the decisive emotional experience of his culminating years. He wanted to take her along on his poetic flights and
wondered whether she would always be so reticent in her verdict
about his latest sonnets in which he believed to have reached a new
level of artistic development. We do not know specifically which
sonnets he is referring to, but some of these reflections in verse of
recent date, which were published, three years later, in *Ich und
Du*, are not easy to understand without knowing their philosophical
background, with which Margareta was not familiar at that time.
Morgenstern must have realized this fact, because the next moment
he accuses himself for being so impatient instead of watching her
grow. In a poem that must have been composed in this period,
which saw an almost daily exchange of letters, the poet pictures the
beloved anxiously waiting to see him:

Nein, dies kann nicht so verbleiben!
Diese Traurigkeit muss enden,
dieses abendliche Wissen

von unsäglich lieben Händen,
die den Herzgeliebten missen,
und statt ihn zu lieben—schreiben.

(*M*, 191)

No, this cannot go on. This sadness must come to an end, this knowing at
dusk of hands dear beyond words that are missing the dearest man and
write to him instead of fondling him.

On October 20, we find Christian on the way to Freiburg, al-
though Margareta tried to head him off with a telegram. He assured
her that it was a small detour on the way to Berlin and that he had
taken along a lot of work which he had to perform for his publisher.
There ensues a pause in Morgenstern's correspondence with Mar-
gareta. Meanwhile he visited her. But her mother decreed that it
was not proper for him to keep on seeing her in her sickroom.
Although this decision seemed incomprehensible to the poet, he
obeyed and journeyed to Strassburg, where he stayed with a friend
from his Breslau days. From Strassburg he sent her an old edition of
the New Testament which he had picked up there and told her that
there is, after Christ, no ultimate greatness except in His spirit.
When she will have truly grasped the Gospel of John, they would
share an innermost secret even if they were never to speak of it (*B*,
November 6, 1908). Morgenstern felt that he should reveal some of
his religious convictions to his beloved. They are those we find
expressed in his "Diary of a Mystic."
The spiritual breakthrough which Morgenstern had experienced
two years before he met Margareta had estranged him somewhat
from his former friends. He realized this and expressed it in these
words: "The deeper a person becomes the more lonesome he gets,
the more even his truest friends leave him alone, out of sensitiveness,
bashfulness, affection, reverence, embarrassment, respect, shyness,
in short, for the best reasons in the world and with unfailing tact of the
heart (*M*, 192). The change from this loneliness to a new togetherness
is described in a poem in *Mensch Wanderer*. It begins

Here is solitude, that was my war cry. The fool I am. The poor soul I am. But perhaps only in this way I preserved myself for you, and for myself, for all of you as the one that I am destined to be . . . I was granted a little adornment here and there, and poison, too, but little more. Thus I became a well-balanced person, a strangely contented one—who was satisfied with everything and nothing, who would float along his way unburdened, for he never committed himself with all he had except to his seriousness, to it alone. Then I met you. Now I'd like to discard that destiny, turn this path bound for the glacier into one that leads to human habitation, I would like to possess and be possessed. (*M*, 196)

Now the poet was convinced that he had found the one friend who would stay with him when the lights of his own life were growing dim. He pleaded with her:

> Lass mich nicht allein, denn es will Abend werden
> und der Tag hat sich geneigt. . . .
> Sieh, wie über aller Erden
> Dunkels Ahnung schon voll Schwermut schweigt. . . .
>
> Alle trachten nun nach ihren Herden,
> deren Glut wie Atem sinkt und steigt—
> o du Brust, die sich zu mir geneigt,
> bleibe mein: denn ich will Abend werden!

> (*M*, 197)

Don't leave me alone, for the evening is drawing near. Behold how over all the land the foreboding of darkness brings a hush fraught with melancholy. They are all anxious for their hearths whose glow sinks and rises like our breathing. Oh heart that has inclined toward me, remain mine, for my evening is drawing near.

The pastoral language of this poem has a Biblical ring. This is not surprising because Morgenstern's love had taken on a religious connotation. Margareta had become a powerful spiritualizing force, and he hoped that this could also be said for him. In the prayer "Getrennter Liebender Gebet zu einander" ("The Separated Lovers Pray to Each Other") contained in *Mensch Wanderer* each plays the role of the guardian angel for the other: "Come to me today, also, stay with me today, also, accompany each one of my steps, sanctify

each step I take. Help me lest I become ensnared and stumble.
Help me to remain strong and beautiful until I again entreat you
next morning. Penetrate me wholly with the light that you are.
Dwell in me as the light does in the air. In order that I may be all
yours, that you may be all mine, this day, also" (*M*, 216). In a more
traditional way, Morgenstern offers a prayer of thanks to the Al-
mighty for His guidance in the past and future. The second stanza of
the sonnet reads:

> Lange Jahre hast Du Dich inmitten
> meines Lebens, ungeahnt, befunden,
> bist mit mir durch Schuld und Not geschritten,
> hast in mir viel Schlimmes überwunden.
>
> Paartest mir zuletzt die rechte Seele,
> dass ich, an ihr schaffend, von ihr wieder
> mitgeschaffen würde, Tag um Tage.
>
> Bleibe bei uns, dass sich Fehl um Fehle
> löse und Ein schwingenstark Gefieder
> uns zu grössern Taten weiter trage.

> (*M*, 224)

For many years Thou hast been in the midst of my life, unsuspected, hast
walked with me through guilt and misery, hast overcome in me much
wickedness. Thou hast given me the right soul to be my spouse in order that
I work on her and, in turn, be worked on by her, day after day. Stay with us
that one flaw after the other be erased and one strong-winged pair of feath-
ers carry us to greater deeds.

The religious tenor of their togetherness is revealed in a short poem
of ten lines published in *Ich und Du*, the collection of lyrics which is
primarily a testimony to the poet's love for Margareta. The poem
describes a wishful dream in which on some star the lovers come to
life again as a blooming rosebush. He is the root, she the bush, he
will be the branches, she the leaves, he the rose, and she its fra-
grance. Thus their lives are united in every fiber, in every breath
rising as a prayer of thanks.[4]

Ich und Du, with the subtitle *Sonette, Ritornelle, Lieder*, published in 1911 has as its motto: "Wer nicht stirbt, vor er stirbt, der verdirbt, wenn er stirbt" ("he who does not die before his death will perish when he dies"). This points out the necessity of a spiritual rebirth during our lifetime. The slender volume begins and ends with a group of sonnets. The ritornello is an Italian verse form with three-line stanzas, but the rhyme scheme varies considerably. Only half of the eight poems grouped together as songs are songs in the strict sense of the word. Perhaps the most beautiful of the sonnets is entitled: "Ein Gleichnis" ("A Parable"). It compares the penetrating power of love to that of the sun's rays. It describes a window which is covered with ice-ferns. These become more and more fragile and finally melt away in the growing strength of the sun's rays.

> . . . der ganzen Sonne liegt der Raum nun offen
> das Glas ward klar und lässt nun ohne Schleier
> den schöpferischen Segen einwärts fluten—
>
> so wehrt, seit deine Liebe mich getroffen,
> mein Sinn, vom Eis der Abwehr täglich freier,
> kaum länger ihren unverwandten Gluten.[5]

Now the room is open to the entire sun, the glass becomes clear and now lets the creative blessing flood inside—thus, ever since your love has struck me my mind, freer every day from the ice of my defense, hardly can ward off any longer its unswerving ardor.

As a counterpart we find, on the opposite page, another parable entitled "Ein Anderes" ("Another One"). In this sonnet we have the graphic description of a forest fire spreading inside the woods like a wildfire, starting with a spark and smoldering in the grass, leaping to the dry branches and falling like a fiery rain of needles from the treetops.

> So fällt die Leidenschaft den Menschen an
> als Spiel zuerst, doch unversehens Ernst,—
> nichts rettet mehr nicht Flucht, nicht Kraft, nicht Stolz.
>
> Du musst sie schaudernd dulden, Weib wie Mann:
> Dass du im Feuertod erkennen lernst,
> wie wild Holz Feuer liebt und Feuer Holz.

Thus passion attacks the human being, first playfully but suddenly in dead earnest, nothing can save him, neither flight, nor strength, nor pride. You must endure it, awestricken, woman as well as man, so that you come to recognize in fiery death how savagely wood loves fire and fire wood.

The spiritualizing trend of Morgenstern's poetry is equally evident in his description of a moonlit landscape. The following ritornello has an extra line in the second stanza, which is expressive of the lingering effect of the ringing of bells.

> Dämmrig blau im Mondenschimmer
> Berge . . . gleich Erinnerungen
> ihrer selbst: selbst Berge nimmer.
>
> Träume bloss noch, hinterlassen
> von vergangnen Felsenmassen:
> So wie Glocken, die verklungen,
> noch die Luft als Zittern fassen.[6]

Mountains shrouded in a dusky bluish haze in the shimmering light of the moon like reminiscences of themselves, no longer mountains. Merely lingering dreams of masses of rocks from bygone days: just like bells no longer ringing, which are felt as vibrations of the air.

The last day of August, 1908, was a memorable one for Morgenstern. The day before he had taken leave of Margareta, and now he wrote his first long letter to her expressing his love. This day remained transfigured in his memory, just as the human race collectively cherished the memory of a golden age reflected in fairy tales and legends. Such a legend is that of Vineta, the submerged city in the North Sea. In Morgenstern's mind it may have stood for the whole submerged continent of Atlantis where, according to old tradition, a prehistoric human culture flourished under divine protection. Rudolf Eppelsheimer pointed out that this Vineta motif appears repeatedly in Morgenstern's work.[7] In the following poem from *Ich und Du* entitled "Ein einunddreissigster August" ("A Thirty-first of August") the legend casts a supernatural aura around this memorable day.

Das war der letzte leuchtende August:
Der Sommer gipfelte in diesem Tage.
Und Glück erklang wie eine Seegrundsage
in den Vinetatiefen unsrer Brust.

Ein leises fernes Läuten kam gegangen—
und welche wollten selbst die Türme sehn,
in denen unsres Glückes Glocken schwangen:
so klar liess Flut und Himmel sie verstehn.

Der Tag versank. Mit ihm Vinetas Stunde.
Septembrisch ward die Welt, das Herz, das Glück.
Ein Rausch nur wie von Tönen blieb zurück
und schwärmt noch über dem verschwiegnen Grunde.

That was the last radiant August. The summer culminated on this day. And happiness echoed like a legend of submerged Vineta in the depth of our heart. A soft distant ringing could be heard—and some even claimed to see the towers in which the bells of our happiness were pealing: so clearly the sky and ocean allowed one to perceive them. The day vanished, and, with it, Vineta's hour. Our world, our heart, our happiness became September-like. An ecstasy as if produced by music was left behind and still hovers over the hushed depth.

In November, 1908, Morgenstern went to Berlin. Margareta followed him a few weeks later. They saw each other almost daily and shared their intellectual and spiritual aspirations. It was this union of their minds and souls that made their mutual affection so wholehearted and profound. Their crowning common experience was to be their acquaintance with Rudolf Steiner's *Geisteswissenschaft (Spiritual Science)* early in 1909. Their common spiritual endeavor is beautifully expressed in the last sonnet of *Ich und Du*.

Nun wollen wir uns still die Hände geben
und vorwärts gehen, fromm, fast ohne Zagen,
und dieses grösste Lebenswagnis wagen:
Zwei miteinander ganz verschlungne Leben.

Und wollen unermüdlich weiterweben
an den für uns nun völlig neuen Tagen
und jeden Abend, jeden Morgen fragen,
ob wir auch ganz Ein Ringen und Ein Streben.

Auch ganz ein unersättlich Langen, Dürsten,
im Mass des Körperlichen, das uns eigen,
uns immer geistiger emporzufürsten:

Dass wir wie Eines Pfeiles Schaft am Schluss,
ineinsverflochten und in einem Schusse
ein neues Reich höhrer Geburt ersteigen.

Now let us quietly extend our hands to each other and go forward, reverent, with scarcely any hesitation, and venture this greatest gamble in life: two lives totally intertwined with each other. And let us continue to weave indefatigably at the days that will now be completely new to us, and ask every evening, every morning whether we have been one united struggle and striving. Really one insatiable reaching and thirsting within the bounds of the bodily existence granted to us, to conquer ourselves rising to ever greater heights, in order that, in the end, we may attain a new realm of spiritual rebirth like the shaft of one arrow forged together in one flight.

CHAPTER 7

Anthroposophy

TWO weeks before he died, Morgenstern dictated from his sick-bed a letter to his publisher concerning the color and design of the cover for his last collection of lyrics, which was to be called *Wir fanden einen Pfad*. These words were taken from the poem which closes the second section of this slender volume. "An den Andern" ("To the Other One") describes how a mountain climber loses his way among the rugged peaks until he meets another one with whom he continues his ascent with renewed courage, and, favored by fate, they find the path to their goal:

> Wir fanden einen Pfad, der klar und einsam
> empor sich zog, bis, wo ein Tempel stand.
> Der Steig war steil, doch wagten wir's gemeinsam. . . .
> Und heut noch helfen wir uns, Hand in Hand.

We found a path which, clear and lonely, made its way up to where a temple stood. The trail was steep, but we ventured on it together, and to this day we help each other, hand in hand.

Morgenstern quotes these lines in his "Autobiographical Note" and adds these words: "The other was *she* who, from that time on, has shared my life. The path was the road to theosophical, an-throposophical knowledge, which is transmitted to us in a unique way by Rudolf Steiner" (S, 13).

Escorted by Morgenstern on her way from Dreikirchen to the station at Waidbruck, Margareta, who was aware of the poet's keen interest in a world of spiritual realities, mentioned Rudolf Steiner to him. In Berlin they attended a lecture by Steiner on Tolstoy and Carnegie in January, 1909. Both, the Russian count and the American millionaire had endeavored to fulfill a modern Christian ideal. The way Steiner compared these two against the background of the history of mankind intrigued Morgenstern and induced him to attend the rest of the lectures. Who was Dr. Steiner? Ten years older than the poet, he had edited Goethe's works on natural science in Kürschner's monumental collection of representative texts from German literature. Then, after laying the philosophical foundation for his work in his *Philosophie der Freiheit (Philosophy of Freedom)* in 1894,[1] he wrote several studies of Goethe, Nietzsche, and Haeckel, as well as two books on mystic trends in Christianity before publishing his *Theosophie (Theosophy)*[2] in 1904. Steiner called his spiritual research *Anthroposophie* to distinguish it from the teachings of the American Theosophical Society whose German section he headed for a number of years. In 1909, an introduction to his method of attaining occult knowledge appeared under the title *Wie erlangt man Erkenntnisse der höheren Welten?* translated as *Knowledge of the Higher Worlds and Its Attainment).*[3]

During the first few months of 1909, Christian and Margareta attended Steiner's biweekly lectures and studied his anthroposophical writings. In April Margareta became a member of the Anthroposophical Society, and the poet wrote to Steiner, asking his permission to accompany her to the forthcoming series of lectures to be delivered in Düsseldorf and Cologne, to which only members were invited. The Düsseldorf cycle on the "Spiritual Hierarchies and Their Reflection in the Physical World" made such a deep impression on Morgenstern that he likewise abandoned all reserve and, in May, joined the Anthroposophical Society. He had now become convinced of man's capacity to reach beyond the phenomenal world and to have metaphysical experience. It was at that time that his longing for such a transcendental breakthrough found expression in one of the most beautiful poems of *Wir fanden einen Pfad:*

> Gib mir den Anblick deines Seins, o Welt. . . .
> Den Sinnenschein lass langsam mich durchdringen. . . .
> So wie ein Haus sich nach und nach erhellt,
> bis es des Tages Strahlen ganz durchschwingen—

und so wie wenn dies Haus dem Himmelsglanz
noch Dach und Wand zum Opfer könnte bringen—
dass es zuletzt von goldner Fülle ganz
durchströmt, als wie ein Geisterbauwerk stände,
gleich einer geistdurchleuchteten Monstranz

So möchte auch die Starrheit meiner Wände
sich lösen, dass dein volles Sein in mein,
mein volles Sein in dein Sein Einlass fände —
und so sich rein vereinte Sein mit Sein.

Just as a house gradually emerges at dawn until it is pervaded entirely by
the rays of the day, and just as if this house could present its very roof and
walls as an offering to the radiance of heaven, so that, in the end, flooded by
golden light throughout, it would stand there like an edifice of the spirits, as
a spiritually transparent monstrance, in the same way let the rigidity of my
walls be dissolved, so that my entire being could enter into your being,
effecting a perfect fusion of one with the other.

Steiner's next series of lectures was scheduled for Oslo. A stipend
provided by Bruno Cassirer made the journey there easier for the
ailing poet. Steiner spoke on Revelation, the last book of the Bible.
In a letter to Margareta, Christian refers to these lectures: "I was
asked recently to have dinner with Dr. Steiner and Fräulein von
Sivers. He spoke very significantly about Nietzsche and Lagarde.
. . . His interpretation of Revelation is grandiose. I shall be happy if
I can digest it together with what has preceded during the summer.
I realize that, for the time being, I must do nothing but study and
again study. Everything else will fall into place. My Berlin friends,
even the dearest ones, will not go along, at first. This I must bear"
(B, May 15, 1909). In the next letter, he told Margareta: [Dr. Stei-
ner] is always extremely kind to me. . . . He is really a great leader,
and it is no disgrace to join him. A boundless, pure spirituality and
spiritual purity emanate from him" (B, May 16). Two days later he
wrote: "What is needed now is not a coddling of the body, but an
unreserved, full-fledged participation in the great new world to
which you have introduced me through Düsseldorf and Koblenz"
(B, May 18). Understandably, Fritz Kayssler viewed Morgenstern's
spiritual activity and the exertions of his travel with misgivings.

Before leaving Oslo, the poet reassured him in a letter: "My condition is excellent. By happy. All this is not so bad. You merely have to find that foundation [source] of healing from which *everything*, from the human nervous system to the public theater, might again be made whole, nay, will certainly renew itself. Such a spiritual foundation I am now beginning to find for myself. If you could only have experienced with me these vistas into the past and future which were opened up here. Let us express our "worship" not on our knees but creatively through our strides" (*B*, May 25).

Morgenstern did not want to miss the convention in Budapest, which began on May 30. This time it was Margareta who felt uneasy about the long railway travel, the unfamiliar food and the hysterical women, in sum, the whole turmoil of an international theosophical convention. The emotional atmosphere was not created by Steiner, who was only one of the speakers. His way of presentation was sobering, strictly matter-of-fact. Again and again, he would warn his listeners not to accept the results of his occult research uncritically. His method, described in his book *Wie erlangt man Erkenntnisse der höheren Welten*, implies a high degree of concentration of the intellectual powers which, in turn, requires a rigorous training of the mind. Steiner's austere precepts inspired Morgenstern's confidence. In *Stufen* we find this self-admonition: "I must learn to concentrate more and more consciously, to overcome all flitting and flickering elements in my mind, to attach a heavy weight to all good thoughts and to every good emotion in order to tie them down. By the same token I must settle down, restrain and control my pace" (*S*, 40). These words are spoken by the poet, not by the man afflicted by a lingering illness. In spite of poverty and disease, Morgenstern now felt favored by a kind of fate and his grateful heart prompted him to be kind and helpful to his fellowmen wherever an opportunity arose. In such a state of mind he wrote: "I take back all the harsh and unkind words that I have ever said in my letters or orally" (*S*, 40).

A person whom he hoped to help was Elisabeth, his father's third wife, who made many people unhappy with her immature and ill-tempered ways. She had written a hateful letter to the poet fifteen months before. The following letter, which Morgenstern sent from Budapest, may have been written to pave the way for a reconciliation. In it he tries to describe to her his new outlook on life. He wrote:

My poetry has as its aim not only to restate and confirm to people what they feel, but—and this would be infinitely more valuable—to give them new feelings. If I don't do it, others will put an end to the continual rehashing of old feelings through their more elevated art and insight, thus providing the possibility of rejuvenation for every soul that wants to be rejuvenated. You'll readily sense that I anticipate such possibilities. But today I'd like to tell you which road I have recognized to be the one that leads to them. It is the road of a purified, if you wish, reborn, spiritualized religion which is not exactly concerned with the official churches but all the more with the great teachers in the evolution of mankind. You have always sensed and known that salvation is not to be found in the materialism of our days. (B, June 10, 1909)

In another letter to Elisabeth, Morgenstern dwells on one important aspect of anthroposophy, the teaching of reincarnation. "Our younger circle had always believed in reincarnation in one way or another, but we had never been given any detailed information, and thus it remained a vague idea without productive power in our lives. Now, at last, the curtain is drawn back and we can, to a certain degree, make our choice whether we, the young and the old, want to stay together in the future stages of the development of our personalities. We shall do so if we unite and stay united in one great effort at achieving ever greater perfection, that is an ever higher capacity of sacrificing ourselves" (B, June 7, 1909). This communion of spirits beyond this life is expressed in a poem from *Wir fanden einen Pfad:*

> Die in Liebe dir verbunden
> werden immer um dich bleiben,
> werden klein und grosse Runden
> treugesellt mit dir beschreiben.
>
> Und sie werden an dir bauen,
> unverwandt, wie du an ihnen,—
> und erwacht zu Einem Schauen,
> werdet ihr wetteifernd dienen!

Those bound to you in love will always be near you, will faithfully form smaller and larger circles together with you. And they will work on you unceasingly just as you will work on them, and awakened to one vision you will vie with each other in serving.

The idea of reincarnation had been familiar to Morgenstern for more than two decades. Now it became a vital part of his religion. We find a number of references to it in *Stufen*. Thus he asks: "Why should this, my life, be a beginning and an end, since nothing is a beginning and an end. Why not simply a continuation, preceded by innumerable entities of the same kind and followed by innumerable such entities" (*S*, 272). A few lines later on, he says: "One understands the human being only—*sub specie reincarnationis*" (*S*, 273).

An integral part of the teaching of reincarnation is the Buddhist doctrine of Karma, the concept that our present life is partly the result of what we have experienced and accomplished in previous incarnations. It is our higher self that leads us into situations where we can build on previous accomplishments or make up for previous transgressions. While bodily characteristics are inherited from our ancestors, the talents with which we are born and which may differ greatly between children of the same parents are the result of our previous incarnations. Since man is free to promote his spiritual development, he can contribute constructively to his future incarnations. All this we find explained in Steiner's *Theosophie*. Morgenstern and his betrothed studied this book closely. They gained a new perspective on the poet's lingering illness. This is revealed in occasional remarks in *Stufen*, such as "Every disease has its special meaning, for every disease is a purification, one only needs to find out from what," or "One should be ashamed of, and rejoice over one's diseases, for they are nothing but transgressions that are being atoned for" (*S*, 151). In a passage dating from 1912, Morgenstern asks: "Do we become sick because our parents were sick or because there is sickness all around us? Or because, for some reason or other, we have prescribed sickness for ourselves in order that it would cure us from something worse, some passion, or some fault, prescribed, before we were born, by a wisdom or insight that was no less individual but, at the same time, much higher than the one of which we are aware in our present incarnation?" (*S*, 281).

The new life referred to in the following poem refers specifically to a future incarnation:

> Überwinde! Jede Stunde
> die du siegreich überwindest,
> sei getrost, dass du im Pfunde
> deines neuen Lebens findest.
>
> Jede Schmach und jede Schande,
> jeder Schmerz und jedes Leiden
> wird bei richtigem Verstande
> deinen Aufstieg mehr entscheiden.[4]

Overcome. Each hour that you overcome successfully, be assured that you will find [it] in the endowment of your new life. Any disgrace and any humiliation, any pain and any suffering, when accepted in the right spirit will enhance your ascent.

Steiner's next series of lectures took place in the last week of June and the first week of July, 1909. It centered around the Gospel of John and its relationship to the other three gospels. Margareta joined the poet in Kassel, where they attended the lectures. At their conclusion, a long conversation between Steiner and Morgenstern established a personal relationship between the two, and the poet addressed the following words to Dr. Steiner, which are recorded in *Stufen:* "I had been walking, as it were, until four o'clock in the morning, and I did not really believe that the world could become much brighter for me. I saw God's light penetrate everywhere, but then you showed me just at the right moment a five o'clock, a six o'clock, a seven o'clock—a new day" (S, 40).

Now Christian and Margareta sought a few weeks of quiet and relaxation in the small village of Kniebis in the Black Forest. Overwhelmed by the new insight into a cosmic Christianity which he had attained in the past few weeks, the poet wrote on a starlit night the famous poem which he later placed at the beginning of *Wir faden einen Pfad:*

O Nacht, du Sternenbronnen,
ich bade Leib und Geist
in deinen tausend Sonnen—
O Nacht, die mich umfleusst
mit Offenbarungswonnen,
ergib mir, was du weisst!
O Nacht, du tiefer Bronnen. . . .

Night, well of stars, I am immersing my body and soul in your thousand
suns. Night, engulfing me in ecstatic revelation, disclose to me what you
know. Night thou deep well. . . .

The secluded life which the poet was leading was in the nature of a
retreat, to use the ecclesiastical term, a period of meditation and
communion with God, to whom he spoke in the following poem:

Nun wohne DU darin,
in diesem leeren Hause,
aus dem der Welt Gebrause
herausfloh und dahin.

Was ist nun noch mein Sinn,—
als dass auf eine Pause,
ich einzig DEINE Klause,
mein Grund und Ursprung bin!

Now, dwell in it, in this empty house from which the turmoil of the world
has fled and gone. What other purpose is there now for me, except that, for
a while, I be Thy abode exclusively, Thou, my origin and foundation.

At the end of August, Morgenstern and Margareta managed to go
to Munich to attend a course of lectures in which Steiner spoke on
the esoteric phase of Asiatic and European religions. While in
Munich, the poet was advised by a lung specialist to return to
Obermais without delay and live a very cautious life. With great
reluctance he accepted the advice and let Margareta attend a later
course by Steiner in Basel on the Gospel of Luke.[5] Morgenstern's
only consolation was that Margareta afterwards gave a detailed re-

port on the lectures. She had also spoken to Dr. Steiner about Christian's health and about his regret that he could not continue at the same pace. Steiner remarked that it would be more beneficial for the poet to absorb what he had learned and let it become productive rather than listening to additional lectures. This was no longer possible anyway because Morgenstern became seriously ill and remained in bed for several weeks while Margareta nursed him with utmost devotion. During the winter months, he translated a play by Knut Hamsun and got *Palmström* and *Einkehr* ready for publication. A wedding that was originally planned for December had to be postponed until spring. The local pastor performed the brief ceremony on March 7. Just a few friends had assembled in the room which the poet had occupied when he first came to Obermais. The upper floor of the villa made a small but comfortable apartment. Morgenstern now started to work with renewed zest until he had a relapse and was bedridden for another few weeks. It was his religious faith that sustained him. He expressed it in these simple lines:

> Du Weisheit meines höhern Ich,
> die über mir den Fittich spreitet
> und mich von Anfang her geleitet,
> wie es am besten war für mich,—
>
> Wenn Unmut oft mich anfocht: nun—
> Es war der Unmut eines Knaben!
> Des Mannes reife Blicke haben
> die Kraft, voll Dank auf Dir zu ruhn.[6]

Thou wisdom of my higher self that spreadest Thy wings over me and hast guided me from the beginning in a way that was best for me,—If I was often tempted by resentment, well, it was the resentment of a boy. The glance of the mature man has the strength to rest upon Thee in gratitude.

In May, 1910, Morgenstern felt strong enough to leave for a higher location. The couple tried a spa near Brixen and Dürrenstein in the Dolomite Mountains, but after a week during which the poet was well and vigorous he suffered a pulmonary attack which forced him to remain in his remote hotel until the end of August. When he learned that Steiner was going to speak on the Gospel of Matthew in Berne,[7] he was eager to go there. Subsequently Christian and Margareta spent a stimulating fall in Munich. The poet still felt vigorous enough to start out on a trip to Sicily, where the two hoped to stay for several months. In Verona, Morgenstern wrote down the following poem, which is included in *Wir fanden einen Pfad*:

> Ich hebe Dir mein Herz empor
> als rechte Gralesschale,
> das all sein Blut im Durst verlor
> nach deinem reinen Mahle,
> o Christ!
>
> O füll es neu bis an den Rand
> mit Deines Blutes Rosenbrand
> dass: DEN fortan ich trage
> durch Erdennächt' und -tage,
> DU bist!

I lift up my heart to Thee as a real chalice of the Grail, which lost all its blood craving for Thy communal feast, oh Christ. Fill it anew to the brim with the rose-fragrant ardor of Thy blood, in order that Thou be the one whom I will bear henceforth through night and day on earth.

The reference to roses in connection with Christ's death probably points to the Rosicrucian tradition, which derives its name from its founder Christian Rosenkreuz.

The voyage on the *Berlin* of the North German Lloyd, sailing from Genoa to Naples and on to Palermo, was favored by sunny weather and was greatly enjoyed by the Morgensterns. They stayed almost two weeks in Palermo, attending two operas and inspecting the cultural treasures of a great past. Then they traveled across the island to the beautifully situated town of Taormina on the strait of Messina, not far from Mount Etna. They rented two rooms for the winter in a Danish boardinghouse. From their windows they could see the ruins of a Greek amphitheater, the sea, and the coast of Italy. Unfortunately, the poet soon discovered that he had overexerted himself. He was to be confined to his bed for five months.

Meanwhile his reputation in Germany had reached a point where two well-known publishers were anxious to obtain the privilege of buying the copyright for all his books, except for the *Galgenlieder*, and to publish all his future productions. Both promised to bring out his complete works. The plan did not materialize. In the spring of 1911 the poet's condition was sufficiently improved for him to leave Taormina. He spent three weeks in the German hospital in Rome, then he journeyed to a newly established sanitarium in Arosa, Switzerland. After staying there for three weeks Christian and Margareta moved to private quarters.

Early in 1912, the poet unexpectedly received an award of one thousand German marks from the Schiller League of German Women. Morgenstern never found out who was instrumental in obtaining this aid for him. He appreciated the sentiment that prompted this gift even more than the real help it represented. He did a good deal of reading and dictated his thoughts in prose and verse to Margareta. At that time he was quite concerned about the spiritual well-being of an old friend of his, Marie Goettling, a very religious, sensitive person, a *Seelenmensch* as the Germans would call her. She found herself in a rut, spiritually speaking, and hoped to receive inspiration from the poet. We have a long letter from him to her which is extremely interesting because it gives an indication of his new view of the Christian faith in contrast to the more orthodox attitude based primarily on religious feeling. He states:

. . . that deep sleep of which you write, could it not be, at the same time, your painful, silent waiting for your, may I say, angel? What is your innermost wish? To be truly needed somewhere, to be indispensible, to be allowed to stake your whole personality in some place. And in such a way that you will be fully appreciated, that you are really in your element. Well, who else needs you but He to whom you have been on the road all your life and who would probably not like to see you set the table in a boardinghouse rather than prepare tables for hungry and lost souls. You yourself have again seen and divined Him in that form in which He now surrounds us. You should strive to reach this transcendental state, but it will not be possible if you place your spiritual hands devoutly and bitterly in your lap and slumber. Where is your place if not among those who let themselves be more and more deeply permeated by Him, but not only in blind faith and out of an instinctive kinship, but more and more consciously with increasing human freedom, increasingly aware of the ways and aims of the spiritual beings that are grouped around Him in an exalted ascending order. Where is your setting except among those who never give up learning. I say all this not in order to arouse you but *because* you had the call and heard it long before I did, because you are really asleep only momentarily, not so much because you were forced to be but rather because you do not have enough confidence. And I would not dare to shake you up so much if I were not convinced that anyone who has a religious past as you have had, during which you not merely believed but searched and tested, accepting new things and making them your own, will not be able to cope with a religious future that is available today whenever and wherever one asks for it. (*B*, January 4, 1912)

In this letter, Morgenstern refers to the angelic hierarchy mentioned in the Bible which Steiner's occult research found to be spiritual realities accessible to the modern mind through appropriate religious training. It is touched upon in a poem from *Wir fanden einen Pfad* which begins:

> Fass es, was sich dir enthüllt'.
> Ahne dich hinan zur Sonne!
> Ahne, welche Schöpfer-Wonne
> jedes Wesen dort erfüllt!
>
> Klimm empor dann dieser Geister
> Stufen bis zur höchsten Schar!
> Und dann endlich nimm Ihn wahr:
> Aller dieser Geister Meister!

Grasp what is revealed to you. Feel your way up to the sun. Divine the creative joy that fills every being there. Ascend the levels of these spirits up to the highest galaxy. And then, finally, catch a glimpse of Him, the master of all these spirits.

The waiting angel, also mentioned in the above letter, is not merely a poetic name for our human conscience; it is, in the anthroposophical view, a spiritual reality referred to in the Christian tradition as the Guardian Angel. Morgenstern describes his nature through the

words which the angel directs to the individual in the poem entitled
"Der Engel" ("The Angel"):

> Wo bist du hin? Noch eben warst du da—
> Was wandtest du dich wieder abwärts, wehe,
> nach jenem Leben, das ich nicht verstehe,
> und warst mir jüngst doch noch so innig nah.
>
> Ich soll hinab mit dir in deine Welt,
> aus der die Schauer der Verwesung hauchen,
> ins Reich des Todes soll ich mit dir tauchen,
> das wie ein Leichnam fort und fort zerfällt?
> . . . .
> Lass mich mein Haupt verhüllen, bis du neu
> mir wiederkehrst, so rein, wie ich dich liebe,
> von nichts erfüllt als süssem Geistestriebe
> und deinem Urbild wieder strahlend treu.

Where have you gone? A moment ago you were here. Alas, why did you
turn away again down to that life that I don't understand, and yet recently
you were so intimately close to me. Am I supposed to descend with you into
your world from which rises the shudder of decay? Am I supposed to plunge
with you into the realm of death which keeps on disintegrating like a
corpse? . . . Let me cover my face until you return to me, restored as pure
as I love you, filled with nothing but the sweet striving for the spirit, and
true again to your original image.

For some time now Morgenstern's vocal cords had been weak-
ened, so that his speech was reduced to a whisper. He hoped
for relief by transferring to a sanitarium in Davos, where the doctor
was an old friend of his. But here he missed his privacy. Quiet and
relaxation were hard to come by in the strictly regulated routine.
However, it was an advantage that the poet was taken care of during
Margareta's absence. She went to Munich to attend anthroposophi-
cal lectures and the performance of one of Steiner's mystery plays.
The poet's letter written to her on August 12, 1912, gives us an
insight into the ideal relationship that existed between the two:

. . . without you I would probably have my mind fixed on the future life, the next life, and the interval between. You are the bond that ties me to the present, that has pulled me back and holds me friendly and lovingly and, as I hope, for the benefit of all of us. You alone, seen in this grand perspective, make this life still so beautiful for me that I shall try hard to share it with you and make it productive for a long time yet. What do brief separations amount to? What will even the great separation amount to some day, since inwardly we shall not leave one another and since we shall find each other outwardly in one way or another, for a continued working together without end?

The poet is thinking here of the anthroposophical view that individuals who are united spiritually for a cause will find ways and means to work together again in future incarnations.

In October Steiner, on his way back from Italy, spent a day with Morgenstern in a Zurich hotel. At that time the poet, who was deeply moved by their conversation, presented his teacher with several of his latest poems. Then he returned to Inner-Arosa, where Margareta rented a small newly built chalet. There they spent the winter months. Along with serious poems and thoughts for his diary, that was to be expanded into an autobiographical novel, the poet wrote some humorous verse for *Palmström*. Realizing the short span of life that was still granted to him, he was determined to extract the greatest value from it by leading a life of inner discipline. In *Stufen* we find the notation: "You are not supposed to covet to be what you are not, but simply to try to do some of your duty day by day. For it is much more difficult to spend one day being truly alert and wide-awake from beginning to end than to spend a year with ambitious intentions and high-flown plans" (S, 170). The second section of *Wir fanden einen Pfad* begins with a short poem that is as striking in its simplicity as in its precept to follow one's conscience:

> Sieh nicht, was andre tun,
> der andern sind so viel,
> du kommst nur in ein Spiel,
> das nimmermehr wird ruhn.
> Geh einfach Gottes Pfad,
> lass nichts sonst Führer sein,
> so gehst du recht und grad,
> und gingst du ganz allein.

Don't mind what the others are doing, there are so many of them, [and] you will get involved in a game that will never come to rest. Simply walk God's path, let nothing else be your guide, then you are walking right and straight, even if you were all by yourself.

Unusually rigorous discipline for himself is reflected in Morgenstern's use of his time when he says: "I can no more write letters than I can engage in conversation. Both make me shallow and leave me in a state of mind whose distaste I would not wish on anyone." In his last years, idle talk became abhorrent to him. This becomes apparent in some passages from *Stufen* and in his verse. In 1912 he wrote: "There is a large number of mental tortures that we employ consciously and subconsciously among and against each other. One of these is asking questions. There are people who want to be questioned as little as possible. Don't misunderstand me: I mean about trivial things. On the other hand, there are people who know hardly any other punctuation but the question mark" (S, 199). What Morgenstern has in mind here is explained in another passage written the year before: "People have sunk so low these days that they are embarrassed to speak about what is essential in their lives and in all life. God, Christ, and immortality are taboo in certain circles as are shirt, pants, and stockings in other circles; the thing to do, the savoir vivre is to ignore them completely. Nowadays only he knows how to live who in fact no longer knows what living means" (S, 278). In the following lines from *Wir fanden einen Pfad* Morgenstern metes out poetic castigation for idle talk:

> Bedenke, Freund, was wir zusammen sprachen.
> War's wert, dass wir den Bann des Schweigens brachen,
> um solche Nichtigkeiten auszutauschen?
>
> So schwätzen wohl zwei Vögel miteinander,
> derweil in unablässigem Gewander
> des Stromes strenge Wogen meerwärts rauschen.

Consider, friend, what we conversed about. Was it worth breaking the rule of silence to exchange such trivialities? Thus two birds might be twittering while in unceasing flow the unrelenting waves of the river press forward toward the ocean.

This is typical for Morgenstern, who was prone to seek the faults of others first of all in himself. He expresses this idea in *Stufen*: "We should grant every person his right, even if it appears to us ever so wrong. We should not give up our fight against this wrong, but we should not wage it outside ourselves, rather in ourselves, against that in ourselves which corresponds to that wrong. Or could we deny that somehow inwardly we have a share in everything evil that happens outside of us? There is enough in us of that which, for instance, arouses in millions of people an enthusiasm for war and induces irresponsible actions—enough in us to rally against us all the vigilance and courage we have" (S, 171). The same idea is expressed in the poem that begins with the following words:

> Was klagst du an
> die böse Welt
> um das und dies?
> bist du ein Mann,
> der niemals Spelt
> ins Feuer blies?
> . . . .
> Was dünkst du dich
> des unteilhaft,
> was Weltbrand nährt!
> Zuerst zerbrich
> die Leidenschaft,
> die dich noch schwärt.
>
> In dich hinein
> nimm allen Zwist
> der Welt sorg nit;
> je wie du rein
> von Schlacke bist
> wird sie es mit.

Why should you accuse the evil world of this and that? Are you a man who never fanned a fire with chaff? . . . . Why do you think you have no share in what feeds the conflagration of the world? First subdue the passion that still festers in you. Overcome all the discord in your own self. Don't mind the world. The purer you become from slack, the purer it will become, too.

The idea that we, as human beings, share the guilt of all fellow-men goes back to Morgenstern's pantheism, to a time when he found this sentiment also expressed in Dostoevski. A passage from *Stufen* states, as early as 1905: "There is no individual guilt, but only collective guilt. We must clearly realize that the punishment of a criminal by our authorities is based only on the appearance of justice, not on justice itself" (S, 140). Such a pantheistic attitude, which blunts the individual accountability, was later revised by Morgenstern through his study of Buddhism and of anthroposophy, which teaches the concept of the balancing of spiritual debts through Karma. It is significant to note that, among the fourteen chapters of *Stufen*, those dealing with ethical concerns, that is, *Ethisches, Erziehung, Selbst-Erziehung* ("discipline," self-discipline"), *Am Tor* ("at the gate") take up considerably more space (from five to twelve pages each) than do the others, written during the last three years of the poet's life. Another facet of Morgenstern's view of divine justice was his restraint in condemning the actions of other human beings and his complete trust in guidance from above. We find this expressed in a companion piece to the poem quoted on page 119 and couched in equally simple language:

> Verlange nichts von irgendwem,
> lass jedermann sein Wesen,
> du bist von irgendwelcher Fehm
> zum Richter nicht erlesen.
>
> Tu still dein Werk und gib der Welt
> allein von deinem Frieden,
> und hab dein Sach auf nichts gestellt
> und niemanden hienieden.

Do not demand anything from anyone, allow everyone his ways. You are not chosen to be the judge by any arbitrary court. Do your work quietly and only share with the world your peace, and rest your cause on nothing and no one on earth.

Helpfulness and kindness are natural manifestations of the mental attitude described above. Concerning kindness, we find this notation in *Stufen*:

Nobody asserts that kindness could not be a weakness, but only the fool says that it must be. He who expects to be thanked for kindness forfeits the most beautiful justification for earning gratitude in the very feeling that he is kind, by considering himself a special benefactor of others, in the awareness of being kind, thus raising himself above the other and feeling superior. Such an expectation, natural and common as it may be, does not only deserve no thanks but exactly that which it is usually rewarded with, a certain indifference, even almost a certain haughtiness that strikes back. He who wants to do good and does not want to go to pieces doing so must get to the point where he considers himself to be a servant of the other, whom a more fortunate fate allows—to compensate for guilt. Far from expecting thanks, he should rather develop a sense of gratitude toward him for giving him the opportunity to help him, irrespective of whether such help will be rewarded subsequently. (*S*, 155)

The ailing poet, when he wrote these lines, was forced to live a rather restricted life. There were not many people to whom he could show his helpfulness. He did not come in daily contact with the domestic help at the sanitarium. His attitude toward them was exceptional, indeed, for the European society of his day. We can infer this from a passage in *Stufen:*

Our servants are not human beings with whom we get together temporarily for our comfort, but rather are they people whom we should serve, if possible, more and better than they serve us. Not in vain and not without meaning must a human being serve physically while the other can, and is allowed to, serve more spiritually. The former must still perform labor and has little insight into the meaning of the difference between all the conditions of life, but we are obligated to work with our minds also for their benefit. We know more about the meaning of life and, therefore, must treat them with as much wisdom and love as we possibly can. We must learn to forgo visible success, just as we must be careful lest we allow them to notice too much our pedagogical intentions. Much that is possible can be done and avoided concerning them if we never lose the regard for the immortal individuality that is hidden in them nor the love toward them as beings that are kindred to us in eternity. (*S*, 128)

Morgenstern's spirit of helpfulness and his sense of gratitude toward all of God's creatures which are assigned to serve us extends beyond the sphere of mankind to the lower realms of creation. Years ago, he had expressed this sympathetic understanding of the animal world in a poem entitled "Mensch und Tier" (*M*, 99). He was at the zoological garden. Many of these captive animals seemed happy and playful, but others had a deathlike stare in their eyes. A silver fox, a wonderfully dainty creature, watched him motionless with a quiet glance. It seemed to resign itself so prudently to its fate, but the poet could read its inner feelings. And then he saw others with similar expressions, and some were restless behind the immobile bars. He trembled with love for them, and his soul felt united with them. Later on, with the help of anthroposophy, he perceived more clearly the universe. Plant life could exist only on the basis of the mineral world, just as the animal world is dependent on vegetation, and mankind could only develop at the expense of the animal kingdom. In a similar way, the spiritual beings beyond the human realm feel their obligation to mankind in the hierarchical order of the universe. The spirit of gratitude that pervades God's whole creation is beautifully expressed in the famous "Die Fusswaschung" ("Maundy").

> Ich danke dir, du stummer Stein
> und neige mich zu dir hernieder:
> Ich schulde dir mein Pflanzensein.
>
> Ich danke euch ihr Grund und Flor,
> und bücke mich zu euch hernieder:
> Ihr halft zum Tiere mir empor.
>
> Ich danke euch, Stein, Kraut und Tier,
> und beuge mich zu euch hernieder:
> Ihr halft mir alle drei zu Mir.
>
> Wir danken dir, du Menschenkind,
> und lassen fromm uns vor dir nieder:
> weil dadurch, dass du bist wir sind.
>
> Es dankt aus aller Gottheit Ein-
> und aller Gottheit Vielfalt wieder.
> In Dank verschlingt sich alles Sein. [8]

I thank you, mute stone, and bend down to you, I owe you my vegetative existence. I thank you, ground and plants, and stoop down to you. You helped me attain the animal state. I thank you, stone, plants, and animals and bow down to you: all three of you helped me to become human. We thank you, member of mankind, and descend to you in pious devotion because we are through your existence. The universe is filled with mutual thanks from all of God's united and manifold manifestations.

If we keep in mind that the German word for humility, *Demut,* is etymologically related to *dienen* and originally indicated the attitude of one who is serving, we can more fully appreciate Morgenstern's statement in the light of the above poem: "Humility is the key to the world. Without it, all knocking, listening, spying is futile" (*S,* 151).

Directly preceding this statement about humility is another equally significant utterance: "There is only one progress, the progress in love, which leads into divine bliss." For Morgenstern this conviction was a natural outgrowth of what he expressed in his poetry from the beginning, that love is the ultimate moving force in the universe. It has found, as the poet subsequently realized, its highest manifestation in Christ. This is expressed in the central stanza of a hymn entitled "Brüder" ("Brothers") written for university students:

> Allen Bruder sein!
> Allen helfen, dienen!
> Ist, seit ER erschienen,
> Ziel allein!

To be a brother to all, to help and serve all is the only goal since His appearance.

More explicit is the poetic expression of this conviction in the poem that follows this hymn in *Wir fanden einen Pfad:*

> Ich habe den MENSCHEN gesehen in seiner tiefsten Gestalt
> ich kenne die Welt bis auf den Grundgehalt.
>
> Ich weiss, dass Liebe, Liebe ihr tiefster Sinn,
> und dass ich da, um immer zu lieben, bin.

Ich breite die Arme aus, wie ER getan,
ich möchte die ganze Welt, wie ER, umfahn.

I have seen man in his deepest manifestation. I know the ultimate quintes-
sence of the world. I know that its deepest meaning is love, love, and that I
am here to love more and more. I am spreading out my arms as He has
done, I would like to embrace the whole world as He did.

In the spring of 1913 Morgenstern traveled to Portorose on the
Adriatic coast, where he spent two happy, productive months.
Upon special request he translated the French poems of Frederick
the Great of Prussia. What made this vacation especially memorable
was the fact that he became acquainted with Michael Bauer, who
was to become his closest friend during the remaining months of his
life. Bauer had been a member of the Theosophical Society for many
years and could enlighten the poet on many aspects of this spiritual
science. In July, when the weather became too hot in Portorose,
Morgenstern went to Bad Reichenhall and, after three weeks, to
Munich for the rest of the year. There he was given special medical
care by Dr. Felix Peipers, at whose home he resided. The highlights
of these weeks were the performance of two of Steiner's mystery
plays[9] and, in connection with these, a series of lectures dealing
with "Die Geheimnisse der Schwelle" ("The Mysteries of the
Threshold").[10] In retrospect, Morgenstern wrote to his friend Kays-
sler concerning these lectures: "There is, in all of today's civilized
world, no greater intellectual treat than to listen to this man, to let
this incomparable teacher deliver lectures to you. Such a course, for
instance, as the present one, my dear man, is the culmination of
European culture of 1913; its like occurs only once and cannot be
repeated" (B, August 24, 1913).

In November the poet, accompanied by Margareta, ventured a
trip to Stuttgart, where Fräulein von Sivers recited a number of
Morgenstern poems from his earlier and more recent periods.
Rudolf Steiner made an introductory speech. It was an occasion of
great joy for Morgenstern who, in spite of constant fever, felt en-
couraged to travel to Leipzig for a course of six lectures. He had a
presentiment that it might be the last opportunity for him to see
Steiner. In a series of lectures given between December 28 and

January 2 the latter spoke on "Christ and the Spiritual World." The impression these lectures made upon the poet may be seen in the following lines:

> Er sprach. Und wie er sprach erschien in ihm
> der Tierkreis, Cherubim und Seraphim,
> der Sonnenstern, der Wandel der Planeten
> von Ort zu Ort.
> Das alles sprang hervor bei seinem Laut,
> ward blitzschnell, wie ein Weltentraum, erschaut,
> der ganze Himmel schien herabgebeten
> bei seinem Wort.[11]

He spoke. And as he spoke the zodiac appeared through him, cherubim and seraphim, the celestial body of the sun, the course of the planets from one place to another. All this sprang into existence through his sound, was envisioned with the speed of lightning, like a world's dream, all the heavens seemed to be called down through his word.

On New Year's Eve, Fräulein von Sivers again recited from Morgenstern's poetry, but this time unpublished poems from *Wir fanden einen Pfad*. A letter to Kayssler of January 10, 1914, expresses the poet's joy over the fact that Kayssler and Michael Bauer had met. The letter says:

Incidentally, these Leipzig days had strange side effects. My temperature which reached 38 degrees [Celsius] began to go down, so that I finally was without fever. Just as strange was what happened to my coughing. Before the Leipzig trip, the urge to cough was often so persistent that I said to myself: it will be quite impossible to attend even one lecture without causing continual disturbances or reaching for stronger doses of codeine. Actually, it turned out that I not only failed to disturb anyone but I practically made no use of my malt lozenges in the course of the evening—in short that no difficulties at all arose for me from this dreaded physical side. If I had yielded, from the start, to my faintheartedness and all the traditional concepts, if I had told myself: no, it won't work, it will be detrimental—in short, if I had entrusted myself to timidity instead of courage I would have reaped the reward for my timidity. I would have continued to spend unhappy days coughing and feeling feverish instead of experiencing my greatest day of honor, to select only one thing (perhaps the least important).

Confirmation of this miraculous momentary improvement in Morgenstern's health during the Leipzig convention is found in the speech which Steiner delivered in memory of the poet shortly after his death: "When I saw him in his room in Leipzig, it was strange to see how healthy, inwardly vigorous this soul was in the decaying body and how well this soul felt in the spiritual life as never before."[12]

In some ways, the Leipzig days were a climax in the poet's inner life. He had arranged to meet some of his close friends from former days. Kayssler reports a month later: "What gave me the greatest joy in Leipzig was that you, my dear old friend, spoke of so many happy and joyous events which you considered as a gain of recent years. The fact that you described these good things so happily made me so happy" (*B*, February 6, 1914). Meanwhile, Morgenstern's physical condition deteriorated and became so precarious that a sanitarium in Arco refused to admit him. In Gries near Bolzano, a sanitarium reluctantly accepted him as a patient. Favored by sunny weather, he spent almost all day lying on the balcony reading and doing some writing. As a judicious reader of newspapers he was convinced that Germany was drifting toward a general collapse. He was distressed to see that Walther Rathenau's book *Zur Mechanik des Geistes (On the Mechanism of the Spirit)* presented a clear diagnosis but offered no remedy. A bright spot in the realm of public life was for him the activity of the Salvation Army. Morgenstern read its history, which had just been published by Diedrichs in Jena. For him this movement constituted a redeeming feature in the annals of modern mankind.

Serious complications set in at the end of February, so that the physician suggested a transfer to the university clinic in Graz, but Margareta preferred some private quarters. After several unsuccessful attempts elsewhere, she rented the upper floor of Villa Helioburg in Untermais near Merano. Michael Bauer, informed of the illness of his friend, interrupted his lecture tour and hurried to his bedside. Together with him, the poet went over the galley proofs of *Wir fanden einen Pfad*, which he dedicated to Rudolf Steiner with these lines:

So wie ein Mensch, am trüben Tag, der Sonne vergisst,—
sie aber strahlt und leuchtet unaufhörlich—
so mag man Dein an trübem Tag vergessen,
um wiederum und immer wiederum
erschüttert, ja geblendet zu empfinden,
wie unerschöpflich fort und fort und fort
Dein Sonnengeist
uns dunklen Wandrern strahlt.

Just as a human being forgets the sun on the dreary day, but it beams and radiates incessantly, just so one may forget you on a gloomy day, only to realize, time and again, deeply moved and even dazzled, how inexhaustibly your sunlike spirit keeps on radiating for us unilluminated wanderers.

We have here, in this slender volume, Morgenstern's spiritual legacy reflecting the religious experience of his last years. Although many of these poems could not have been written without anthroposophical insight, almost all is expressed in such terms that it is readily accessible to any person, whatever his religious persuasion may be. We learn, for instance, that others can help us find the path to ultimate truth but that the last decisive steps must be taken by the individual himself. This involves rigorous training of our willpower, of our trains of thought, and of our moods.

Geschöpf nicht mehr, Gebieter der Gedanken,
des Willens Herr, nicht mehr in Willens Frone,
der flutenden Empfindung Mass und Meister.

No longer creature, but master of our thoughts, in command of our will, no longer in its servitude, moderating and controlling our fluctuating emotions.

Real depth and the distant truth can only be reached by "ein tiefdemütig lebenslanges Lernen" ("real humility and lifelong learning"). You may, for a long time, grope in the dark for the doorlatch. When you find it and open the door, you will turn white as a sheet "und wie ein Leichnam hinfällt, wird/dein Leib hinfallen in den Sand" ("and like a corpse your body will fall down in the sand"). Thus the poet describes the overwhelming reaction to an experience

in the spiritual sphere. More joyous, more intimate and more
ethereal is the description from "Hymne":

> Wie ein Atmen ganz im Licht
> ist es, wie ein schimmernd Schweben. . . .
> Himmels-licht—in Deinem Leben
> lebten je wir, je wir nicht?
>
> Konnten fern von Dir verziehen,
> flohen Dich, verbannt, verdammt?
> Doch in Deine Harmonien
> kehren heim, die Dir entstammt.

Like breathing immersed entirely in light, it is like a shimmering floating.
. . . Light of Heaven—did we ever live in Thy life, or didn't we? Could we
tarry far from Thee, evade Thee, banished and condemned? But we who
descend from Thee return home to Thy harmonies.

The role which, according to anthroposophy, the hierarchies are
playing in the spiritual world, and the central cosmic significance of
Christ's life on earth (from His baptism by John the Baptist to His
death on the cross) for the history of this planet is beautifully
expressed in the poem entitled "Licht ist Liebe" ("Light is Love"):

> Licht ist Liebe . . . Sonnen-Weben
> Liebes-Strahlung einer Welt
> schöpferischer Wesenheiten—
>
> die durch unerhörte Zeiten
> uns an ihrem Herzen hält,
> und die uns zuletzt gegeben
>
> ihren höchsten Geist in eines
> Menschen Hülle während dreier
> Jahre: da ER kam in Seines
>
> Vaters Erbteil—nun der Erde
> innerlichstes Himmelsfeuer:
> dass auch sie einst Sonne werde.

Light is love . . . creative activity of the sun, love radiating from a world of creative beings which through time immemorial has held us close to its heart and which has finally given us its highest spirit in the body of a human being during three years, when He came into His Father's own—now the earth's innermost heavenly fire in order that it, too, may become sunlike some day.

Morgenstern did not feel disturbed by his approaching death. When, a short time before his death, someone inquired about his illness, he replied that he did not feel sick, that only a person who is a slave to his illness is actually ill. No really free human being could be sick. In his own case his works could bear this out.

He passed away in the early morning hours of the last day of March. Margareta was with him, and his last glance filled with love and gratitude was directed at her. Michael Bauer, who was in his room down the hall, had a vision of the poet's death. "His whole bed was flooded with light," he said.[13] Christian Morgenstern left this world willingly, facing the world to come in a spirit of humility, as is evident from this poem in *Wir fanden einen Pfad*:

> Da nimm. Das lass ich dir zurück, o Welt. . . .
> Es stammt von dir. Es sei von neuem dein.
> Da, wo ich jetzo will hinaus, hinein,
> bin ich nicht mehr auf dich gestellt.
> Da gilt der blasse Geist allein,
> den ich mir formte über dir
> ach nur wie einen blassen Opferrauch,—
> da gilt nur der, ach so schwache Hauch,
> der von dem CHRISTUS lebt in mir.

Take it. This I leave behind for you, world. It comes from you. Let it be yours anew. Where I am about to go away and into I have no need of you any more. There the pale spirit alone counts which I built above you, also, only like a thin smoke rising from the sacrificial offering—there only the ever-so-weak spirit counts that lives in me from Christ.

Cremation took place in Basel on April 4. The urn with Morgenstern's ashes was later placed in the Goetheanum, the visible center of the Anthroposophical Movement in Dornach near

Basel, Switzerland. With Margareta Morgenstern and Michael Bauer as editors, the poet's posthumous works were published by Piper, notably the *Stufen, eine Entwicklung in Aphorismen und Tagebuch-Notizen (Stages, a Development in Aphorisms and Diary Notes,* 1918), *Epigramme und Sprüche (Epigrams and Maxims,* 1920), and *Mensch Wanderer, Gedichte aus den Jahren 1887–1914 (Man the Pilgrim, Poems from the Years 1887–1914,* 1927). In reference to these, Albert Soergel says: "They open up Morgenstern's entire world of thought, they present the development of a personality equally significant from the human and artistic points of view, they draw a picture of one of the few entirely pure human beings, a profound religious searcher, the most sincere believer in Christ in an age of unbelievers, a warning conscience in shallow days."[14]

CHAPTER 8

Conclusion

THE articles which appeared in the German and Swiss press[1] commemorating the centenary of Morgenstern's birth in May, 1971, emphasized his grotesque humor as his special contribution to the history of German literature, in its continuing effectiveness and as a forerunner of the present predilection for the absurd. The enthusiastic reception of the *Galgenlieder* on the part of the general public encouraged the poet to cultivate his gift for this kind of humor. Palmström and von Korf gradually took the place of the gallows fellows and remained a ferment in the poet's mind until the very end of his relatively short life. An essential expression of Morgenstern's sovereign free spirit, he himself did not consider this humorous poetry the main vehicle of his poetic mission. He called the *Galgenlieder* and *Palmström* "Beiwerke" ("minor works"). His main effort was devoted to his serious lyrics. How does he compare in this field to the three most famous poets of his day? With Stefan George (1868–1933) he shared the firm conviction of the sacredness of his own poetic mission, but an increasing sense of humility[2] fortunately forestalled the self-righteous literary conceit that eventually froze George's artistic accomplishments, while Morgenstern remained receptive to new ever deeper experiences. As to Hugo von Hofmannsthal (1874–1929), some of Morgenstern's poems attained the bewitching melodiousness of the young Austrian in the facile manner of his early verse. Rilke (1875–1926) surpassed Morgenstern in the exquisite artistry of poetic expression, but the latter's lyrics seem more sincere and less contrived. Both poets, in their search for ultimate values, had suprasensible experiences of a metaphysical world and conveyed them in their last lyrics, Rilke in an idiom all his own, Morganstern in a more easily accessible language.[3]

133

In the photographic realism advocated by some of his literary contemporaries Morgenstern saw not an artistic goal but a means of bringing out the purely human qualities of a person beset by the hardships of his daily life. He shared with the budding early expressionists their concern for the preservation of humanity in a mechanistic era. He also shared their religious fervor, but he expressed it with a sincerity of conviction that was less ostentatious and more quietly enduring.

It is the earnestness and caliber of his thinking that raises Morgenstern above all other poets of German neo-romanticism, with the exception of Rilke and possibly of the later Hofmannsthal. After the early long-lasting confrontation with Nietzsche, after the intimate acquaintance with Ibsen's criticism of the contemporary social order with its pseudomorality, after the study of Lagarde's far-reaching political views, Morgenstern started a relentless search for ultimate truth. He became acquainted with Spinoza's pantheism and Meister Eckhart's profound mysticism, as well as with the idealistic philosophy of Fichte and Hegel. He went beyond Western thought in his study of Buddhism, which reinforced his early belief in reincarnation, known to him through Schopenhauer's philosophy. Thus Morgenstern came to believe in the eternal self and its unity with God, while most of his "progressive" contemporaries accepted the materialistic views of modern science. The most powerful impact was made on him by the Gospel of John, which reveals Christ as the most perfect manifestation of God's presence in man and of the divine destiny of mankind. The enormous wealth of thought absorbed, and more or less digested, by the poet who, according to his own admission, was no systematic thinker, found clarification and fulfillment in the teachings of Rudolf Steiner. In perilous physical condition Morgenstern devoted the last five years of his life to the study and poetic presentation of anthroposophy, a *Weltanschauung* for which he had unknowingly prepared himself so well in his independent search for truth.

Fredrich Hiebel, the editor of the anthroposophical weekly *Das Goetheanum*, has pointed out[4] that on the occasion of the poet's centenary the press extolled Morgenstern's grotesque humor at the expense of his serious poetry, which is described as too delicately fanciful in the traditional neo-romantic vein, afflicted with a gentle melancholy and a spirituality which is said to be too elusive for the present mind. Contrary to this view, which would relegate Morgenstern's serious lyrics to a literary fashion in vogue at the turn of the century and to an esoteric creed accessible to a selected few, I should like, in conclusion, to offer evidence that Morgenstern's total reputation has become more and more widespread during the past four decades.

As mentioned in the previous chapter, important posthumous works of his appeared before and during the 1920s. In 1929, *Auswahl (Selection)*, the first important selection from Morgenstern's serious lyrics, was made by his widow and Michael Bauer. The 1930s saw the appearance of two smaller collections by the same editors: *Meine Liebe ist gross wie die Welt (My Love Embraces the World*, 1936) and *Wer vom Ziel nicht weiss, kann den Weg nicht haben (He who does not Know about the Goal cannot find the Road*, 1939), which was arranged by Margareta Morgenstern as a vade mecum for every day of the year. In 1940 the Insel-Verlag included a selection of Morgenstern lyrics in the *Insel–Bücherei* under the title *Zeit und Ewigkeit (Time and Eternity)*. The same publisher brought out *Alle Galgenlieder*, including *Palmström, Palma Kunkel*, and *Gingganz*, in 1944. The increasing popularity of the eclectic pocketbook editions in the 1940s is felt in the publication of four different collections, two by Piper, *Stilles Reifen (Quiet Maturing*, 1945) and *Man muss aus einem Licht fort in das andere gehn (One should Progress from One Light into the Next*, 1949), and two in Switzerland, *Flugsand und Weidenflöten (Quick Sand and Shepherds' Pipes)* and *Ausgewählte Gedichte (Selected Poems)*, both published in 1945. Meanwhile, an Italian translation of portions of *Stufen* had appeared in Milan: *Aforismi di mistica a ricerca spirituale* (1942), and a French translation of twenty gallows songs came out in Paris under the title *Pierrot pendu* (1948). Morgenstern wrote some children's songs which the Oldenburg Verlag brought out in an illustrated song book in 1943. There were only a few new publications in the 1950s. Piper published a new selection of humorous verse: *Egon und Emilie* in 1950, selected aphorisms entitled *Vom offenbaren Geheimnis* in 1954 and other poems, simply called *Gedichte (Poems)* in 1959. The Insel-Verlag added two more volumes to the Insel–Bücherei: *Palmström* (1956) and *Briefe (Letters)* in 1957. Previously an English translation of some *Galgenlieder* by E. W. Eitzen had appeared in the Insel-Verlag (1953). The Italian translation was entitled *Palma Conochia* (1958).

A veritable Morgenstern revival set in during the 1960s, possibly spurred by the fiftieth anniversary of the poet's death. It began with *Der Spielgeist, Verse und Prosa (The Playful Spirit,* 1960). Piper published an enlarged edition of *Horatius Travestitus* in 1961 with Latin and German on opposite pages; and, in the following year, Morgenstern's collected letters, which Margareta edited under the title *Alles um des Menschen willen (Everything for the Sake of Humanity).* The Deutscher Taschenbuch Verlag brought out pocket-book editions of *Palmström* (1961), *Galgenlieder* (1962), and *Stufen* (1962). *Dich führt der Weg (The Road will Lead You)* is the title of selected religious poems by Morgenstern published in 1964. The same year brought *Eine Auswahl der schönsten Galgenlieder in deutscher und englischer Sprache,* translated by Albert Roy with drawings by Martin Koble, and *Christian Morgenstern's Galgenlieder,* a selection translated, with an introduction, by Max Knight. A selection from Morgenstern's work called *Das Schönste aus seinem Werk,* as well as *Gesammelte Werke in einem Band (Collected Works in One Volume)* appeared in 1965. The same year saw a publication of *Palmström* with woodcuts by Hans Peter Willberg, a collection called *Morgensternchen (Little Morning Stars),* selected by Erich Seemann, and a translation of selected Morgenstern poems into Latin *Carmina Lunovilia* with a Latin-German vocabulary appended. English translations of gallows songs by Reinhold Seligmann appeared in 1966, and those by W. D. Snodgrass and Lore Segal in 1967. Unfortunately, only a few serious poems by Morgenstern have been published in English translation, scattered in English anthologies of German poetry.[5] Morgenstern's complete original works began to appear in 1971 in a handsome seventeen-volume edition which is now almost complete. Additional volumes will contain his translations.

Notes and References

Preface

1. August Closs, *The Genius of the German Lyric* (London, 1965), p. 315.

2. Michael Bauer, *Christian Morgensterns Leben und Werk* (Munich, 1933).

3. Martin Beheim-Schwarzbach, *Christian Morgenstern in Selbstzeugnissen und Bilddokumenten* (Hamburg, 1964).

4. *The Gallows Songs. Christian Morgenstern's "Galgenlieder,"* trans. Max Knight. (Berkeley, 1964).

Chapter One

1. See Rudolf Steiner, *Christian Morgenstern: Der Sieg des Lebens über den Tod* (Dornach, 1935), p. 31.

2. Christian Morgenstern, *Stufen,* ed. Margareta Morgenstern (Munich, 1918), p. 26; hereafter cited in text as *S*.

3. Letter of August 30, 1893, in Christian Morgenstern, *Gesammelte Briefe* (Munich, 1962); hereafter cited in text as *B*.

Chapter Three

1. Christian Morgenstern, *Gesammelte Werke in einem Band* (Munich, 1965), p. 65.

2. Bauer, p. 139.

3. Ibid., p. 159.

Chapter Four

1. Bauer, pp. 180–83.

2. *The Gallows Songs,* trans. Max Knight (Berkeley, 1964), p. 47. Literal translation: "Fraternal Song of the Gallows Brothers": Life's horrible entanglement, we dangle here from the red thread, the croaker croaks, the spider spins and the wind strokes our drooping heads. . . . The hoot owl hoots its hoo hoo hoos. There it dawns, it brews, it blues.

3. Ibid., p. 49. Literal translation: "The Hanged Man's Song to Sophia, the Hangman's Maid": Sophia, my hangman's lass, come, kiss my skull. My mouth, it is true, is a black abyss—but you are good and noble. Sophia, my hangman's lass, come, stroke my skull. My head, it is true, is without hair—but you are good and noble. Sophia, my hangman's lass, come, peer into my skull. The eagle, is it true, has picked my eyes—but you are good and noble.

4. Ibid., p. 89. Literal translation: "The Vulture-Lamb": The lamb-vulture [*Lämmergeier*] is well known, the vulture-lamb is named here for the first time. The vulture is obvious, but the lamb is mealy-mouthed. It does not cry, it does not bleat, but when you get close, it eats you. Then it sends a pious glance to Heaven and everybody just loves it.

5. Ibid., p. 83. Literal translation: A dejected donkey one day said to his wedded spouse: "I am so dumb, you are so dumb, come, let us die." But as it often turns out, the two continued to live merrily.

6. Ibid., p. 91. Literal translation: On a calendar leaf on the wall a lion is portrayed. He looks at you moved and quietly the whole seventeenth of April. Thus he likes to remind you that he at least still exists.

7. Ibid., p. 79. Literal translation: "The Chicken": In the railway station not built for it a chicken walks back and forth. Where is the stationmaster? Will they not harm the chicken? Let's hope so. Let us say emphatically that we sympathize with it, even in this place where it has no right to be.

8. Ibid., p. 33. Literal translation: "Two Funnels": Two funnels saunter through the night./Through the narrow shaft of slender trunks,/does flow white moonlight/soft and serene/upon their/forest path/and so/forth.

9. Ibid., p. 147. Literal translation: Korf invents a daynight lamp which transforms even the brightest day into night, as soon as it is turned on. When he demonstrates it at the footlights of the convention hall, no one who knows his field can fail to recognize that we are confronted with—it gets dark in the broadest daylight and a storm of applause goes through the house, and they call for the janitor Mampe to turn on the light—that we are confronted with the fact that the above-mentioned lamp, when turned on, actually transforms even the brightest day into night.

10. Ibid., p. 19. Literal translation: A weasel sat on a pebble in the midst of a rippling brook. Do you know why? The mooncalf revealed it to me. The sneaky beast did it for the sake of the rhyme.

Chapter Five

1. Rudolf Eppelsheimer, in *Gedenkausgabe 1871–1971* (Stuttgart, 1971), p. 33.

2. Ibid., p. 29.

3. Bauer, p. 175.

4. Christian Morgenstern, *Epigramme und Sprüche,* ed. Margareta Morgenstern (Munich, 1919), p. 111.

5. Christian Morgenstern, *Einkehr* (Munich, 1910), p. 16.

Chapter Six

1. *Einkehr,* p. 87.

2. *Einkehr,* p. 59.

3. Eppelsheimer, p. 32.

4. Christian Morgenstern, *Ich und Du* (Munich, 1911), p. 60.

5. Ibid., p. 26.

6. Ibid., p. 43.

7. Eppelsheimer, p. 18.

Chapter Seven

1. *The Philosophy of Freedom* (London, 1964).

2. *Theosophy* (London, 1954).

3. London, 1963.

4. Christian Morgenstern, *Wir fanden einen Pfad* (Munich, 1914), p. 21.

5. See Rudolf Steiner, *The Gospel of St. Luke: Ten Lectures Given in Basel* (London, 1964).

6. *Wir fanden einen Pfad,* p. 28.

7. Rudolf Steiner, *The Gospel of St. Matthew* (London, 1946).

8. *Wir fanden einen Pfad,* p. 55.

9. Rudolf Steiner, *Mystery Plays,* trans. H. Collins et al. (London, 1925).

10. Rudolf Steiner, *Secrets of the Threshold, a Course of eight Lectures* (New York, 1928).

11. Eppelsheimer, p. 87.

12. Rudolf Steiner, *Christian Morgensterns Leben und Werk* (Dornach, 1935), p. 67.

13. Bauer, p. 370.

14. Quoted by Bauer, p. 76.

Chapter Eight

1. *Frankfurter Allgemeine Zeitung, Süddeutsche Zeitung, Badische Zeitung, Berner Tagblatt, Basler Nachrichten, Neue Zürcher Zeitung.*

2. Friedrich Hiebel, "Die Demut in der Dichtung Christian Morgensterns," *Germanic Review* 22 (1947), 55–71.

3. Erich Hofacker, "R. M. Rilke und Christian Morgenstern," *Proceedings of the Modern Language Association* 50 (1935), 606–14.

4. *"Das Goetheanum," Wochenschrift für Anthroposophie*, July 11, 1971.

5. John Rothensteiner, *A German Garden of the Heart: German Lyrics from the Volkslied unto Rainer Maria Rilke* (St. Louis, 1934); and Angel Flores, *An Anthology of German Poetry from Hölderlin to Rilke in English Translation* (New York, 1960).

Selected Bibliography

PRIMARY SOURCES

1. First Editions

In Phanta's Schloss: Ein Cyclus humoristisch-phantastischer Dichtungen. Berlin: Cassirer, 1895.

Horatius travestitus: Ein Studentenscherz. Berlin: Cassirer, 1897.

Auf vielen Wegen: Gedichte. Berlin: Cassirer, 1897.

Ich und die Welt: Gedichte. Berlin: Cassirer, 1897.

Ein Sommer: Verse. Berlin: Cassirer, 1900.

Und aber ründet sich ein Kranz. Berlin: Cassirer, 1902.

Galgenlieder. Berlin: Cassirer, 1905.

Melancholie: Neue Gedichte. Berlin: Cassirer, 1906.

Palmström. Berlin: Cassirer, 1910.

Einkehr: Gedichte. Munich: Piper, 1910.

Ich und Du: Sonette, Ritornelle, Lieder. Munich: Piper, 1911.

Wir fanden einen Pfad: Neue Gedichte. Munich: Piper, 1914.

Palma Kunkel. Berlin: Cassirer, 1916.

Stufen: Eine Entwicklung in Aphorismen und Tagebuch-Notizen. Edited by Margareta Morgenstern. Munich: Piper, 1918.

Der Gingganz. Edited by Margareta Morgenstern. Berlin: Cassirer, 1918.

Epigramme und Sprüche. Edited by Margareta Morgenstern. Munich: Piper, 1919.

Klein Irmchen: Ein Kinderbuch. Illustrated by Josua L. Gampp. Berlin: Cassirer, 1921.

Über die Galgenlieder. Berlin: Cassirer, 1921.

Mensch Wanderer: Gedichte aus den Jahren 1887–1914. Edited by Margareta Morgenstern. Munich: Piper, 1927.

Die Schallmühle: Grotesken und Parodien. Edited by Margareta Morgenstern. Munich: Piper, 1928.

2. Later Editions

Kindergedichte. Munich: Carl Ueberreuter, 1965.

141

Versammlung der Nägel: Grotesken und Parodien. Munich: Piper, 1969.

Gedenkausgabe 1871–1971. Selected and with an introduction by Rudolf Eppelsheimer. Stuttgart, 1971.

Sämtliche Dichtungen. Basel: Zbinden, 1971–. This edition will include Morgenstern's translations; volume 15 appeared in 1977.

Alle Galgenlieder. With vignettes by Christian Morgenstern. Frankfurt: Insel, 1972.

Galgenlieder: Der Gingganz. 11th ed. Munich: Deutscher Taschenbuch Verlag, 1973.

Gesammelte Werke in einem Band. 11th ed. Munich: Piper, 1974.

Palmström: Palma Kunkel. 8th ed. Munich: Deutscher Taschenbuch Verlag, 1974.

Das grosse Christian-Morgenstern-Buch. Edited by Michael Schulte. Munich: Piper, 1976.

3. Translations by Morgenstern

AUGUST STRINDBERG: *Inferno.* Berlin: Georg Bondi, 1898.

HENRIK IBSEN: *Das Fest auf Solhaug.* In *Sämtliche Werke in deutscher Sprache,* vol. 2. Berlin: Fischer, 1898.

———. *Komödie der Liebe.* Ibid., vol. 3. Berlin: Fischer, 1898.

———. *Wenn wir Toten erwachen.* Ibid., vol. 9. Berlin: Fischer, 1899.

———. *Brand.* Ibid., vol. 4. Berlin: Fischer, 1901.

———. *Peer Gynt.* Ibid., vol. 4. Berlin: Fischer, 1901.

———. *Gedichte.* Ibid., vol. 1. Berlin: Fischer, 1903.

———. *Catalina.* Ibid., vol. 1. Berlin: Fischer, 1903.

Knut Hamsun. *Abendröte.* Munich: Albert Langen, 1904.

———. *Spiel des Lebens.* Munich: Albert Langen, 1910.

Friedrich der Grosse. *Werke.* Edited by Gustav Berthold Volz. vol. 10. Berlin: Verlag des Preussischen Staatsarchivs, 1914.

4. Letters

Ein Leben in Briefen. Edited by Margareta Morgenstern. Wiesbaden: Insel, 1952.

Alles um des Menschen willen: Gesammelte Briefe. Selected with postscript by Margareta Morgenstern. Munich: Piper, 1962.

5. Translations into English

The Moonsheep. Translated by A. E. W. Eitzen. Wiesbaden: Insel, 1953.

The Gallows Songs. Christian Morgenstern's "Galgenlieder." Translated by Max Knight. Berkeley: University of California Press, 1964.

Eine Auswahl der schönsten Galgenlieder in deutscher und englischer

Sprache. Translated by Albert Roy, with drawings by Martin Koblo. Wiesbaden: Insel, 1964.

Gallows Songs. Translated by W. D. Snodgrass and Lore Segal. Ann Arbor: University of Michigan Press, 1967.

The Daynight Lamp and other Poems. Translated by Max Knight. Boston: Houghton Mifflin, 1973.

SECONDARY SOURCES

1. Books and Dissertations

BAUER, MICHAEL. *Christian Morgensterns Leben und Werk.* Completed by Margareta Morgenstern in collaboration with Rudolf Meyer. Munich: Piper, 1933.

BEHEIM-SCHWARZBACH, MARTIN. *Christian Morgenstern in Selbstzeugnissen und Bilddokumenten.* Hamburg: Rowohlt, 1964.

DIETERICH, PAULA. "Weltanschauungsentwickelung in der Lyrik Christian Morgensterns," Ph.D. dissertation, University of Cologne, 1926.

EPPELSHEIMER, RUDOLF. *Mimesis und Imitatio Christi bei Loerke, Däubler, Morgenstern, Hölderlin.* Berne: Francke, 1968.

FORSTER, LEONARD W. *Poetry of Significant Nonsense.* Cambridge: Bowes & Bowes, 1962.

GEIGER, PAUL. "Mystik und Reinkarnation bei Christian Morgenstern." Ph.D. dissertation, University of Heidelberg, 1941.

GERATHS, FRANZ. "Christian Morgenstern, sein Leben und sein Werk." Ph.D. dissertation, University of Munich, 1926.

GIFFEI, HERBERT. "Christian Morgenstern als Mystiker." Ph.D. dissertation, University of Berne, 1931.

GRODDEK, MARIE. *Henrik Ibsen, der Fragesteller, und Christian Morgenstern, der Antwortgeber.* Berne: Troxler, 1957.

GUMTAU, HELMUT. *Christian Morgenstern.* Berlin: Colloquium, 1971.

HIEBEL, FRIEDRICH. *Christian Morgenstern. Wende und Aufbruch unseres Jahrhunderts.* Berne: Francke, 1957.

KLEMM, GÜNTHER. "Die Liebeslyrik Christian Morgensterns und ihre Bedeutung." Ph.D. dissertation, University of Bonn, 1933.

MACK, ALBERT. "Christian Morgensterns Welt und Werk." Ph.D. dissertation, University of Zurich, 1930.

MARTIN, BERNHARD. "Christian Morgensterns Dichtungen nach ihren mystischen Elementen." Weimar: Duncker, 1931.

MAZUR, RONALD. "The Late Lyric Poetry of Christian Morgenstern." Ph.D. dissertation, University of Michigan, 1975.

MEYER, RUDOLF. *Christian Morgenstern in Berlin.* Stuttgart: Urachhaus, 1959.

STEFFEN, ALBERT. *Vom Geistesweg Christian Morgensterns.* Dornach: Verlag für schöne Wissenschaften, 1971.

STEINER, RUDOLF. *Christian Morgenstern: Der Sieg des Lebens über den Tod.* Edited by Marie Steiner. Dornach: Philosophisch-Anthroposophischer Verlag am Goetheanum, 1935.

WALTER, JÜRGEN. *Sprache und Spiel in Christian Morgensterns Galgenliedern.* Freiburg: Alber, 1966.

2. Articles

BÖKENKAMP, W. "Christian Morgenstern, poète d'humour surréaliste." *Revue des lettres modernes* 1 (1954), 1–18.

HIEBEL, FRIEDRICH. "Die Demut in der Dichtung Christian Morgensterns." *Germanic Review* 22 (1947), 55–71.

HOFACKER, ERICH. "Christian Morgenstern als Mystiker." *Journal of English and German Philology* 27 (1928), 200–216.

———. "Novalis und Christian Morgenstern" *Germanic Review* 6 (1931), 373–388.

———. "R. M. Rilke und Christian Morgenstern." Proceedings of the Modern Language Association 50 (1935), 606–614.

———. "Ruhe und Aufstieg im Werk Christian Morgensterns." *Monatshefte* 52 (1960), 49–6.

———. "Zur Naturlyrik Christian Morgensterns." *Monatshefte* 39 (1947), 421–38.

KLEMPERER, VICTOR. "Christian Morgenstern und der Symbolismus." *Zeitschrift für Deutschkunde* 42 (1928), 39–55, 124–36.

SCHÖNFELD, HERBERT. "Über Christian Morgensterns Grotesken." *Zeitschrift für deutsche Bildung* 8 (1932), 225–37.

WIRTH, OTTO. "Christian Morgenstern." *Monatshefte* 34 (1942), 64–79.

ZOEST, AART J. A. VAN. "Eine semiotische Analyse von Morgensterns Gedicht Fisches Nachtgesang.'" *Zeitschrift für Literatur und Linguistik* 16 (1974), 49–67.

Index

146

WORKS

(Poems are given below the title of the collection. The titles to poems are indicated by capitalization; the remaining references are to first lines.)